50 Sugar-Free Desserts for Kids Recipes for Home

By: Kelly Johnson

Table of Contents

- Sugar-Free Chocolate Avocado Pudding
- Lemon Yogurt Popsicles
- Almond Flour Banana Muffins
- Raspberry Chia Seed Pudding
- Coconut Flour Pancakes
- Greek Yogurt Berry Parfait
- Sugar-Free Apple Cinnamon Muffins
- Avocado Chocolate Mousse
- Strawberry Nice Cream
- Carrot Cake Energy Bites
- Sugar-Free Blueberry Cheesecake Bars
- Chocolate Zucchini Bread
- Peanut Butter Chocolate Chip Cookies (with sugar substitute)
- Vanilla Almond Milk Panna Cotta
- No-Bake Peanut Butter Oat Bars
- Kiwi Lime Sorbet
- Cinnamon Baked Pears
- Sugar-Free Pumpkin Pie
- Chocolate Chip Zucchini Muffins
- Blackberry Coconut Chia Popsicles
- Coconut Macaroons (sweetened with stevia)
- Mango Coconut Rice Pudding
- Sugar-Free Lemon Bars
- Spinach Banana Muffins
- Avocado Lime Ice Cream
- Peanut Butter Banana "Nice" Cream
- Blueberry Almond Flour Coffee Cake
- No-Bake Almond Butter Bars
- Raspberry Coconut Milk Rice Pudding
- Chocolate Covered Strawberries (using sugar-free chocolate)
- Vanilla Chia Seed Pudding
- Sugar-Free Oatmeal Raisin Cookies
- Pumpkin Spice Energy Balls
- Watermelon Sorbet
- Orange Creamsicles (made with unsweetened coconut milk)

- Almond Butter Chocolate Cups
- Sugar-Free Lemon Loaf Cake
- Berry Crumble Bars (using sugar-free sweetener)
- Chocolate Chip Chickpea Blondies
- Matcha Coconut Bliss Balls
- Peanut Butter Banana Ice Cream Sandwiches
- Blueberry Almond Flour Scones
- No-Bake Coconut Cream Pie
- Mango Lime Sorbet
- Sugar-Free Banana Bread
- Avocado Key Lime Pie
- Chocolate Almond Flour Waffles
- Raspberry Coconut Milk Ice Cream
- Vanilla Bean Cheesecake Bites
- Lemon Coconut Energy Bites

Sugar-Free Chocolate Avocado Pudding

Ingredients:

- 2 ripe avocados
- 1/4 cup unsweetened cocoa powder
- 1/4 cup sugar-free sweetener (such as erythritol or stevia), adjust to taste
- 1 teaspoon vanilla extract
- 1/4 cup almond milk or coconut milk (unsweetened)
- Pinch of salt

Instructions:

Cut the avocados in half, remove the pits, and scoop out the flesh into a blender or food processor.
Add cocoa powder, sugar-free sweetener, vanilla extract, almond milk, and a pinch of salt to the blender.
Blend until smooth and creamy, scraping down the sides of the blender or processor as needed to ensure everything is well combined.
Taste and adjust sweetness if necessary by adding more sweetener.
Transfer the pudding to serving dishes or bowls.
Chill in the refrigerator for at least 30 minutes before serving to allow the pudding to set.
Serve chilled and enjoy your delicious sugar-free chocolate avocado pudding!

This pudding is rich, creamy, and decadent without any added sugar, making it a perfect guilt-free dessert option. You can also top it with fresh berries, chopped nuts, or a dollop of whipped coconut cream for extra flavor and texture.

Lemon Yogurt Popsicles

Ingredients:

- 1 cup plain Greek yogurt
- 1/4 cup fresh lemon juice
- Zest of 1 lemon
- 1/4 cup sugar-free sweetener (such as erythritol or stevia), adjust to taste
- 1 teaspoon vanilla extract
- Optional: Lemon slices or mint leaves for garnish

Instructions:

In a mixing bowl, combine the Greek yogurt, fresh lemon juice, lemon zest, sugar-free sweetener, and vanilla extract. Mix well until smooth and creamy.
Taste the mixture and adjust sweetness according to your preference by adding more sweetener if needed.
Pour the mixture into popsicle molds, leaving a little space at the top for expansion.
Insert popsicle sticks into each mold.
If desired, garnish each popsicle with a thin lemon slice or a small mint leaf.
Place the popsicle molds in the freezer and let them freeze for at least 4-6 hours, or until completely firm.
Once frozen, remove the popsicles from the molds by running the molds under warm water for a few seconds to loosen them.
Serve immediately and enjoy these delightful sugar-free Lemon Yogurt Popsicles on a hot day!

These popsicles are creamy, tangy, and bursting with lemon flavor. They make a perfect guilt-free treat for both kids and adults alike. Feel free to experiment with different variations, such as adding crushed berries or using lime juice instead of lemon for a twist!

Almond Flour Banana Muffins

Ingredients:

- 2 cups almond flour
- 1 teaspoon baking powder
- 1/2 teaspoon baking soda
- 1/4 teaspoon salt
- 3 ripe bananas, mashed
- 3 large eggs
- 1/4 cup coconut oil, melted
- 1 teaspoon vanilla extract
- Optional: Sugar-free sweetener (such as erythritol or stevia), to taste
- Optional add-ins: Chopped nuts, dark chocolate chips, or cinnamon

Instructions:

Preheat your oven to 350°F (175°C). Line a muffin tin with paper liners or grease with cooking spray.
In a large mixing bowl, whisk together the almond flour, baking powder, baking soda, and salt.
In another bowl, mash the ripe bananas until smooth. Add the eggs, melted coconut oil, and vanilla extract. Mix until well combined.
If desired, add sugar-free sweetener to the wet mixture for added sweetness, adjusting to taste.
Pour the wet ingredients into the dry ingredients and stir until just combined. Be careful not to overmix.
If using any add-ins like chopped nuts, dark chocolate chips, or cinnamon, gently fold them into the batter.
Spoon the batter evenly into the prepared muffin tin, filling each muffin cup almost to the top.
Bake in the preheated oven for 20-25 minutes, or until the tops are golden brown and a toothpick inserted into the center of a muffin comes out clean.
Remove from the oven and allow the muffins to cool in the tin for a few minutes before transferring them to a wire rack to cool completely.
Once cooled, enjoy these moist and flavorful Almond Flour Banana Muffins as a delightful sugar-free snack or breakfast treat!

These muffins are naturally sweetened by ripe bananas and have a wonderful almond flavor from the almond flour. They are gluten-free, low-carb, and perfect for anyone looking for a healthier baked treat without added sugars.

Raspberry Chia Seed Pudding

Ingredients:

- 1 cup fresh or frozen raspberries
- 2 tablespoons sugar-free sweetener (such as erythritol or stevia), adjust to taste
- 1/2 teaspoon vanilla extract
- 1/4 cup chia seeds
- 1 cup unsweetened almond milk or coconut milk

Instructions:

In a blender or food processor, combine the raspberries, sugar-free sweetener, and vanilla extract. Blend until smooth.
In a mixing bowl, combine the raspberry puree with chia seeds and unsweetened almond milk or coconut milk.
Stir well to combine all ingredients thoroughly.
Taste the mixture and adjust sweetness if needed by adding more sugar-free sweetener.
Cover the bowl and refrigerate for at least 2 hours, or preferably overnight, to allow the chia seeds to absorb the liquid and thicken the pudding.
Stir the pudding mixture occasionally during the chilling time to prevent clumping.
Once the chia seeds have absorbed the liquid and the pudding has reached a thick consistency, give it a final stir.
Serve the Raspberry Chia Seed Pudding in bowls or glasses, and optionally, garnish with fresh raspberries or sliced almonds.
Enjoy this nutritious and satisfying sugar-free dessert as a healthy snack or breakfast option!

This Raspberry Chia Seed Pudding is packed with fiber, omega-3 fatty acids, and antioxidants from the raspberries and chia seeds. It's naturally sweet and makes a great guilt-free treat for anyone looking to enjoy a sugar-free dessert.

Coconut Flour Pancakes

Ingredients:

- 4 large eggs
- 1/2 cup coconut milk (or any milk of choice)
- 1/4 cup coconut oil, melted (or butter)
- 1 teaspoon vanilla extract
- 1/4 cup coconut flour
- 1 tablespoon granulated sweetener (such as erythritol or sugar)
- 1/2 teaspoon baking powder
- Pinch of salt

Instructions:

Prepare Batter: In a mixing bowl, whisk together the eggs, coconut milk, melted coconut oil (or butter), and vanilla extract until well combined.
Combine Dry Ingredients: In a separate bowl, whisk together the coconut flour, granulated sweetener, baking powder, and a pinch of salt.
Mix Wet and Dry Ingredients: Gradually add the dry ingredient mixture to the wet ingredients, stirring until there are no lumps and the batter is smooth. Let the batter sit for a few minutes to thicken slightly.
Cook Pancakes: Heat a non-stick skillet or griddle over medium heat and lightly grease with additional coconut oil or butter.
Pour Batter: Spoon about 2 tablespoons of batter onto the skillet for each pancake, spreading it slightly with the back of the spoon to form a round shape.
Cook Until Bubbles Form: Cook the pancakes for about 2-3 minutes, or until bubbles start to form on the surface and the edges look set.
Flip and Cook Other Side: Carefully flip the pancakes and cook for an additional 1-2 minutes on the other side, or until golden brown and cooked through.
Repeat: Continue cooking the remaining batter in batches, adding more coconut oil or butter to the skillet as needed.
Serve: Serve the coconut flour pancakes warm with your favorite toppings, such as fresh berries, sliced bananas, maple syrup, honey, or a dollop of Greek yogurt.
Enjoy: Enjoy these delicious and fluffy coconut flour pancakes as a nutritious and satisfying breakfast or snack!

These pancakes are gluten-free, grain-free, and lower in carbs compared to traditional pancakes. They have a subtle coconut flavor and pair beautifully with a variety of toppings. Customize them to your liking and savor a delightful and healthy breakfast!

Greek Yogurt Berry Parfait

Ingredients:

- 1 cup Greek yogurt (plain or vanilla flavored)
- 1 cup mixed berries (such as strawberries, blueberries, raspberries)
- 1/4 cup granola
- 1 tablespoon honey (optional)
- Fresh mint leaves for garnish (optional)

Instructions:

Prepare the Berries: Wash and dry the berries. If using strawberries, remove the stems and slice them into smaller pieces if desired.
Layer the Parfait:
- Start by spooning a layer of Greek yogurt into the bottom of a glass or bowl.
- Add a layer of mixed berries on top of the yogurt.
- Sprinkle a layer of granola over the berries.

Repeat Layers:
- Repeat the layers of Greek yogurt, berries, and granola until the glass or bowl is filled or until you've used up all the ingredients.

Drizzle with Honey (Optional):
- If desired, drizzle a little honey over the top of the parfait for added sweetness.

Garnish (Optional):
- Garnish the parfait with fresh mint leaves for a pop of color and extra freshness.

Serve Immediately:
- Serve the Greek Yogurt Berry Parfait immediately and enjoy as a nutritious breakfast, snack, or dessert.

Variations:
- Feel free to customize your parfait by adding other ingredients such as sliced bananas, chopped nuts, coconut flakes, or a sprinkle of cinnamon.

Enjoy: This Greek Yogurt Berry Parfait is a delicious and healthy treat that's packed with protein from the Greek yogurt, vitamins from the berries, and crunch from the granola. It's perfect for starting your day or as a refreshing snack!

Feel free to adjust the quantities of ingredients based on your preferences and serving size. Get creative with different types of berries and toppings to make this parfait your own. Enjoy the delightful flavors and textures of this easy and nutritious Greek Yogurt Berry Parfait!

Sugar-Free Apple Cinnamon Muffins

Ingredients:

- 2 cups almond flour
- 1/4 cup coconut flour
- 1 teaspoon baking powder
- 1/2 teaspoon baking soda
- 1 teaspoon ground cinnamon
- 1/4 teaspoon salt
- 3 large eggs
- 1/2 cup unsweetened applesauce
- 1/4 cup melted coconut oil or butter
- 1 teaspoon vanilla extract
- 2 medium apples, peeled, cored, and finely diced
- Optional: Chopped nuts or seeds for topping (e.g., walnuts, pecans, or pumpkin seeds)

Instructions:

Preheat Oven: Preheat your oven to 350°F (175°C). Line a muffin tin with paper liners or grease with coconut oil or butter.

Mix Dry Ingredients: In a large bowl, whisk together the almond flour, coconut flour, baking powder, baking soda, ground cinnamon, and salt.

Combine Wet Ingredients: In another bowl, whisk together the eggs, unsweetened applesauce, melted coconut oil (or butter), and vanilla extract.

Mix Wet and Dry Ingredients: Pour the wet ingredients into the bowl of dry ingredients and stir until well combined and no flour clumps remain.

Fold in Diced Apples: Gently fold in the finely diced apples into the muffin batter.

Fill Muffin Tin: Divide the muffin batter evenly among the prepared muffin cups, filling each about 3/4 full.

Add Toppings (Optional): Sprinkle chopped nuts or seeds on top of each muffin for added texture and flavor.

Bake Muffins: Bake in the preheated oven for 20-25 minutes, or until the tops are golden brown and a toothpick inserted into the center of a muffin comes out clean.

Cool and Serve: Allow the muffins to cool in the muffin tin for 5 minutes, then transfer them to a wire rack to cool completely.

Enjoy: These Sugar-Free Apple Cinnamon Muffins are perfect for a healthy breakfast or snack option. They are naturally sweetened by the applesauce and apples, making them suitable for a sugar-free diet.

Feel free to customize these muffins by adding your favorite spices such as nutmeg or cloves, or by incorporating other mix-ins like raisins or shredded coconut. Store any leftovers in an airtight container in the refrigerator for up to several days, or freeze for longer storage. Enjoy these delicious and nutritious muffins guilt-free!

Avocado Chocolate Mousse

Ingredients:

- 2 ripe avocados
- 1/2 cup unsweetened cocoa powder
- 1/2 cup almond milk (or any milk of choice)
- 1/4 cup maple syrup or honey (adjust to taste)
- 1 teaspoon vanilla extract
- Pinch of salt
- Optional toppings: Fresh berries, sliced bananas, chopped nuts, shredded coconut

Instructions:

Prepare Avocados: Cut the avocados in half, remove the pits, and scoop out the flesh into a blender or food processor.
Add Remaining Ingredients: Add the unsweetened cocoa powder, almond milk, maple syrup (or honey), vanilla extract, and a pinch of salt to the blender or food processor with the avocados.
Blend Until Smooth: Blend all the ingredients together until smooth and creamy, scraping down the sides of the blender or food processor as needed to ensure everything is well combined.
Taste and Adjust Sweetness: Taste the chocolate mousse and adjust the sweetness to your liking by adding more maple syrup or honey if desired.
Chill (Optional): For a thicker and chilled mousse, transfer the mixture to a bowl and refrigerate for about 30 minutes to 1 hour.
Serve: Divide the avocado chocolate mousse into serving bowls or glasses.
Add Toppings (Optional): Garnish with fresh berries, sliced bananas, chopped nuts, or shredded coconut, if desired.
Enjoy: Serve and enjoy this creamy and decadent Avocado Chocolate Mousse as a healthy dessert or snack!

This avocado chocolate mousse is rich, smooth, and naturally sweetened with maple syrup or honey. It's a nutritious alternative to traditional chocolate mousse and is packed with healthy fats from the avocados. Feel free to customize the sweetness and toppings according to your taste preferences. This dessert is perfect for satisfying chocolate cravings while being dairy-free and vegan-friendly!

Strawberry Nice Cream

Ingredients:

- 2 cups frozen strawberries
- 1-2 ripe bananas, frozen and sliced
- 1/2 cup unsweetened almond milk (or any milk of choice)
- 1-2 tablespoons honey or maple syrup (optional, adjust to taste)
- 1 teaspoon vanilla extract

Instructions:

Prepare Frozen Fruits: Ensure that both the strawberries and bananas are frozen. If not already frozen, slice the bananas and place them in a single layer on a baking sheet lined with parchment paper. Freeze until solid.
Blend Ingredients: In a blender or food processor, combine the frozen strawberries, frozen banana slices, almond milk, honey or maple syrup (if using), and vanilla extract.
Blend Until Smooth: Blend the mixture until smooth and creamy, stopping occasionally to scrape down the sides of the blender or food processor.
Adjust Sweetness (Optional): Taste the nice cream and add more honey or maple syrup if you prefer a sweeter flavor.
Serve Immediately: Scoop the strawberry nice cream into bowls and serve immediately for a soft-serve consistency.
Optional Firming: For a firmer texture, transfer the nice cream to a container and freeze for about 1-2 hours before serving. Allow it to soften slightly at room temperature before scooping.
Enjoy: Enjoy this delicious and refreshing strawberry nice cream as a healthier alternative to traditional ice cream!

Variations:

- Add-ins: Feel free to add other ingredients to customize your nice cream, such as a handful of fresh berries, a scoop of protein powder, a tablespoon of nut butter, or a sprinkle of chocolate chips.
- Toppings: Serve your strawberry nice cream with toppings like sliced strawberries, chopped nuts, granola, or shredded coconut for added flavor and texture.

This strawberry nice cream is naturally sweet, creamy, and dairy-free, making it a perfect guilt-free treat. It's also a great way to use up ripe bananas and frozen strawberries. Enjoy this refreshing dessert or snack during warm weather or anytime you crave a fruity, creamy indulgence!

Carrot Cake Energy Bites

Ingredients:

- 1 cup rolled oats
- 1/2 cup shredded carrots
- 1/4 cup chopped nuts (such as pecans or walnuts)
- 1/4 cup raisins or chopped dried apricots
- 1/4 cup creamy almond butter or peanut butter
- 1/4 cup honey or maple syrup
- 1 teaspoon vanilla extract
- 1 teaspoon ground cinnamon
- 1/4 teaspoon ground nutmeg
- Pinch of salt
- Optional: Shredded coconut for rolling

Instructions:

Combine Ingredients: In a large mixing bowl, combine the rolled oats, shredded carrots, chopped nuts, and raisins or dried apricots.

Add Wet Ingredients: Add the almond butter or peanut butter, honey or maple syrup, vanilla extract, ground cinnamon, ground nutmeg, and a pinch of salt to the bowl.

Mix Well: Mix all the ingredients together until well combined and the mixture starts to stick together.

Chill Mixture (Optional): For easier rolling, you can chill the mixture in the refrigerator for about 30 minutes.

Roll into Balls: Using your hands, roll the mixture into small balls, about 1-inch in diameter.

Optional Coating: If desired, roll the energy bites in shredded coconut for an extra touch.

Store: Place the carrot cake energy bites in an airtight container and refrigerate for up to one week.

Enjoy: Enjoy these delicious and nutritious carrot cake energy bites as a quick snack or post-workout fuel!

Notes:

- Feel free to customize these energy bites by adding ingredients like chia seeds, flaxseed meal, or protein powder for extra nutrition.
- You can adjust the sweetness by adding more or less honey or maple syrup according to your preference.
- These energy bites are a great portable snack and a healthier alternative to store-bought snacks. They are packed with fiber, protein, and natural sweetness from the carrots and dried fruit.

These carrot cake energy bites capture the flavors of a classic carrot cake in a convenient bite-sized form. They are perfect for satisfying your sweet tooth while providing a boost of energy and nutrition. Enjoy making and snacking on these delicious treats!

Sugar-Free Blueberry Cheesecake Bars

Ingredients:

For the Crust:

- 1 cup almond flour
- 1/4 cup melted coconut oil or butter
- 2 tablespoons powdered erythritol (or sweetener of choice)
- 1/2 teaspoon vanilla extract
- Pinch of salt

For the Cheesecake Filling:

- 16 oz (2 packages) cream cheese, softened
- 1/2 cup powdered erythritol (or sweetener of choice)
- 2 large eggs
- 1 teaspoon vanilla extract
- Zest of 1 lemon
- 1 cup fresh or frozen blueberries

Instructions:

Preheat Oven: Preheat your oven to 350°F (175°C). Line an 8x8-inch baking dish with parchment paper, leaving some overhang for easy removal.

Make the Crust:
- In a mixing bowl, combine the almond flour, melted coconut oil or butter, powdered erythritol, vanilla extract, and a pinch of salt.
- Stir until well combined and press the mixture evenly into the bottom of the prepared baking dish.

Bake the Crust: Bake the crust in the preheated oven for 10 minutes. Remove from the oven and set aside to cool slightly.

Prepare the Cheesecake Filling:
- In a large mixing bowl, beat the softened cream cheese and powdered erythritol until smooth and creamy.
- Add the eggs, one at a time, beating well after each addition.
- Stir in the vanilla extract and lemon zest until fully incorporated.

Assemble the Cheesecake Bars:
- Pour the cheesecake filling over the cooled crust in the baking dish.
- Scatter the blueberries evenly over the top of the cheesecake filling.

Bake the Cheesecake Bars:
- Return the baking dish to the oven and bake for 30-35 minutes, or until the edges are set and the center is slightly jiggly.

Cool and Chill:
- Allow the cheesecake bars to cool completely in the baking dish at room temperature.
- Once cooled, refrigerate for at least 2 hours (or overnight) to set.

Slice and Serve:
- Use the parchment paper overhang to lift the cheesecake bars out of the baking dish.
- Slice into squares and serve chilled.

Enjoy: These sugar-free blueberry cheesecake bars are creamy, decadent, and bursting with juicy blueberries. They make a delicious keto-friendly dessert or snack option!

Notes:

- Feel free to substitute the blueberries with other berries such as raspberries or blackberries if desired.
- Adjust the sweetness to your liking by adding more or less powdered erythritol or using your preferred sweetener.
- Store any leftovers in an airtight container in the refrigerator for up to several days.

These sugar-free blueberry cheesecake bars are perfect for anyone looking to enjoy a creamy and indulgent dessert without the added sugar. They are low-carb, keto-friendly, and sure to satisfy your sweet cravings!

Chocolate Zucchini Bread

Ingredients:

- 1 1/2 cups grated zucchini (about 1 medium zucchini)
- 1 cup all-purpose flour
- 1/2 cup unsweetened cocoa powder
- 1 teaspoon baking powder
- 1/2 teaspoon baking soda
- 1/2 teaspoon salt
- 1/2 cup granulated sugar
- 1/2 cup brown sugar
- 2 large eggs
- 1/2 cup vegetable oil or melted coconut oil
- 1 teaspoon vanilla extract
- 1/2 cup chocolate chips (semi-sweet or dark chocolate), plus more for topping (optional)

Instructions:

Preheat Oven: Preheat your oven to 350°F (175°C). Grease or line a 9x5-inch loaf pan with parchment paper.

Prepare Zucchini: Grate the zucchini using a box grater. Place the grated zucchini on a clean kitchen towel or paper towels, and squeeze out excess moisture. Set aside.

Mix Dry Ingredients: In a medium bowl, whisk together the flour, cocoa powder, baking powder, baking soda, and salt until well combined.

Mix Wet Ingredients: In a large bowl, whisk together the granulated sugar, brown sugar, eggs, vegetable oil (or melted coconut oil), and vanilla extract until smooth.

Combine Wet and Dry Ingredients: Gradually add the dry ingredient mixture to the wet ingredients, stirring until just combined. Avoid over-mixing.

Add Zucchini and Chocolate Chips: Gently fold in the grated zucchini and chocolate chips into the batter until evenly distributed.

Pour into Loaf Pan: Pour the batter into the prepared loaf pan, spreading it out evenly.

Optional Topping: Sprinkle additional chocolate chips on top of the batter if desired.

Bake: Bake in the preheated oven for 50-60 minutes, or until a toothpick inserted into the center comes out clean (with a few moist crumbs attached).

Cool and Serve: Allow the chocolate zucchini bread to cool in the pan for about 10-15 minutes, then transfer it to a wire rack to cool completely before slicing.

Enjoy: Slice and enjoy this delicious chocolate zucchini bread as a snack or dessert!

Notes:

- This chocolate zucchini bread can be stored in an airtight container at room temperature for up to 3-4 days, or in the refrigerator for longer shelf life.
- Feel free to add chopped nuts (such as walnuts or pecans) to the batter for extra crunch and flavor.
- You can also make muffins using this batter. Simply divide the batter among muffin cups and adjust the baking time accordingly (about 20-25 minutes for muffins).

This chocolate zucchini bread is a wonderful way to enjoy a moist and chocolatey treat while sneaking in some veggies! It's great for using up garden-fresh zucchini and makes a delightful snack or dessert for any occasion. Enjoy baking and savoring this delicious bread!

Peanut Butter Chocolate Chip Cookies (with sugar substitute)

Ingredients:

- 1 cup creamy peanut butter (unsweetened)
- 1/2 cup granulated sugar substitute (such as erythritol or monk fruit sweetener)
- 1 large egg
- 1 teaspoon vanilla extract
- 1/2 teaspoon baking soda
- 1/4 teaspoon salt
- 1/2 cup sugar-free chocolate chips

Instructions:

Preheat Oven: Preheat your oven to 350°F (175°C). Line a baking sheet with parchment paper or silicone baking mat.
Mix Wet Ingredients: In a mixing bowl, combine the creamy peanut butter, granulated sugar substitute, egg, and vanilla extract. Mix until smooth and well combined.
Add Dry Ingredients: Add the baking soda and salt to the peanut butter mixture. Mix until incorporated.
Fold in Chocolate Chips: Gently fold in the sugar-free chocolate chips until evenly distributed throughout the dough.
Form Cookie Dough Balls: Scoop tablespoon-sized portions of cookie dough and roll them into balls. Place them on the prepared baking sheet, leaving some space between each cookie.
Flatten Cookie Dough Balls (Optional): Use a fork to create a crisscross pattern on each cookie dough ball, gently flattening them.
Bake Cookies: Bake in the preheated oven for 10-12 minutes, or until the edges are golden brown.
Cool and Serve: Allow the cookies to cool on the baking sheet for a few minutes before transferring them to a wire rack to cool completely.
Enjoy: Once cooled, enjoy these delicious sugar-free peanut butter chocolate chip cookies as a guilt-free treat!

Notes:

- Ensure that your peanut butter is creamy and well-stirred before using it in the recipe.

- You can adjust the sweetness by adding more or less of the sugar substitute according to your preference.
- Feel free to substitute the sugar-free chocolate chips with chopped nuts or cacao nibs for added texture and flavor.
- Store any leftover cookies in an airtight container at room temperature for several days, or freeze for longer storage.

These sugar-free peanut butter chocolate chip cookies are perfect for those looking to reduce sugar intake while still enjoying a classic cookie flavor. They are easy to make and satisfy cravings for something sweet and comforting. Enjoy baking and indulging in these delicious cookies!

Vanilla Almond Milk Panna Cotta

Ingredients:

- 2 cups unsweetened almond milk
- 1/4 cup granulated sugar or sugar substitute (adjust to taste)
- 1 teaspoon vanilla extract
- 2 teaspoons powdered gelatin
- 2 tablespoons cold water
- Sliced almonds, for garnish (optional)
- Fresh berries, for serving (optional)

Instructions:

Prepare Gelatin: In a small bowl, sprinkle the powdered gelatin over the cold water. Let it sit for about 5 minutes to bloom.
Heat Almond Milk: In a saucepan, heat the almond milk and granulated sugar (or sugar substitute) over medium heat. Stir occasionally until the mixture is hot but not boiling, and the sugar has dissolved.
Add Vanilla Extract: Remove the saucepan from the heat and stir in the vanilla extract.
Dissolve Gelatin: Add the bloomed gelatin to the warm almond milk mixture. Stir until the gelatin is completely dissolved.
Pour into Molds: Divide the mixture evenly among serving glasses or ramekins.
Chill: Refrigerate the panna cotta for at least 4 hours, or until set.
Garnish and Serve: Before serving, garnish with sliced almonds and fresh berries if desired.
Enjoy: Serve and enjoy this delightful vanilla almond milk panna cotta as a light and creamy dessert!

Notes:

- For a richer flavor, you can substitute some or all of the almond milk with coconut milk or heavy cream.
- Adjust the sweetness to your preference by adding more or less sugar or sugar substitute.

- To unmold the panna cotta easily, briefly dip the bottom of the ramekins or glasses in warm water before running a knife around the edge and inverting onto a serving plate.

This vanilla almond milk panna cotta is a dairy-free and delicious dessert that's perfect for those looking for a lighter alternative to traditional panna cotta. It's smooth, creamy, and infused with a lovely vanilla flavor. Enjoy making and serving this elegant dessert for any occasion!

No-Bake Peanut Butter Oat Bars

Ingredients:

- 1 cup creamy peanut butter (unsweetened)
- 1/2 cup honey or maple syrup
- 1/2 cup coconut oil, melted
- 3 cups old-fashioned oats
- 1 teaspoon vanilla extract
- 1/4 teaspoon salt
- 1/2 cup mini chocolate chips (optional)

Instructions:

Prepare Pan: Line an 8x8-inch square baking pan with parchment paper, leaving some overhang for easy removal.

Combine Peanut Butter, Honey, and Coconut Oil: In a microwave-safe bowl or on the stovetop, combine the creamy peanut butter, honey or maple syrup, and melted coconut oil. Heat in short intervals (if using microwave) or over low heat (if using stovetop), stirring frequently until smooth and well combined.

Add Oats, Vanilla, and Salt: Stir in the old-fashioned oats, vanilla extract, and salt until evenly coated.

Add Chocolate Chips (Optional): If using, fold in the mini chocolate chips until distributed throughout the mixture.

Press into Pan: Transfer the mixture to the prepared baking pan. Use a spatula or your hands to press it evenly into the pan.

Chill: Place the pan in the refrigerator for at least 2 hours, or until firm and set.

Slice and Serve: Lift the bars out of the pan using the parchment paper overhang. Slice into bars or squares.

Enjoy: Serve and enjoy these delicious no-bake peanut butter oat bars as a wholesome snack or dessert!

Notes:

- You can customize these bars by adding chopped nuts, dried fruit, or seeds to the mixture.
- Store the bars in an airtight container in the refrigerator for up to one week, or freeze for longer storage.

- If the mixture seems too dry, you can add more peanut butter, honey, or coconut oil to achieve the desired consistency.

These no-bake peanut butter oat bars are easy to make and require minimal effort. They are perfect for satisfying sweet cravings and providing a quick energy boost. Enjoy the combination of peanut butter, oats, and honey in these delicious homemade bars!

Kiwi Lime Sorbet

Ingredients:

- 6 ripe kiwis, peeled and chopped
- Zest and juice of 2 limes
- 1/2 cup granulated sugar (adjust to taste)
- 1/2 cup water

Instructions:

Prepare Simple Syrup: In a small saucepan, combine the granulated sugar and water. Heat over medium heat, stirring occasionally, until the sugar has dissolved completely. Remove from heat and let it cool completely.
Blend Kiwi and Lime: In a blender or food processor, combine the chopped kiwis, lime zest, lime juice, and cooled simple syrup. Blend until smooth.
Strain (Optional): For a smoother sorbet, strain the mixture through a fine-mesh sieve to remove any kiwi seeds or pulp.
Chill: Transfer the mixture to a shallow dish or container. Cover and refrigerate for at least 1-2 hours, or until thoroughly chilled.
Churn in Ice Cream Maker (Optional): If you have an ice cream maker, churn the chilled mixture according to the manufacturer's instructions until it reaches a sorbet-like consistency.
Freeze Without Ice Cream Maker: If you don't have an ice cream maker, transfer the chilled mixture to a freezer-safe container. Place it in the freezer and stir every 30 minutes for about 2-3 hours, or until it firms up to a sorbet consistency.
Serve: Once the sorbet reaches the desired consistency, scoop into bowls or glasses.
Garnish (Optional): Garnish with lime slices or kiwi slices for a decorative touch.
Enjoy: Serve and enjoy this refreshing and tangy kiwi lime sorbet as a light and fruity dessert!

Notes:

- Adjust the sweetness of the sorbet by adding more or less sugar, depending on the sweetness of the kiwis.
- For a more intense lime flavor, you can add extra lime zest or juice to suit your taste.

- Store any leftover sorbet in a covered container in the freezer. Let it sit at room temperature for a few minutes before serving if it becomes too firm.

This kiwi lime sorbet is a delightful treat that's perfect for cooling down on a hot day. It's bursting with the bright and zesty flavors of kiwi and lime, making it a refreshing and satisfying dessert option. Enjoy making and savoring this homemade sorbet!

Cinnamon Baked Pears

Ingredients:

- 4 ripe but firm pears (such as Bosc or Anjou)
- 2 tablespoons unsalted butter, melted
- 2 tablespoons honey or maple syrup
- 1 teaspoon ground cinnamon
- 1/4 teaspoon ground nutmeg
- 1/4 teaspoon vanilla extract
- Optional: Chopped nuts (such as walnuts or pecans) for garnish
- Optional: Vanilla ice cream or whipped cream for serving

Instructions:

Preheat Oven: Preheat your oven to 375°F (190°C).
Prepare Pears: Wash and dry the pears. Cut each pear in half lengthwise and use a spoon to scoop out the seeds and core, creating a hollow in the center.
Arrange Pears in Baking Dish: Place the pear halves cut-side up in a baking dish or on a rimmed baking sheet lined with parchment paper.
Mix Cinnamon Mixture: In a small bowl, combine the melted butter, honey or maple syrup, ground cinnamon, ground nutmeg, and vanilla extract. Stir until well combined.
Brush Pears with Cinnamon Mixture: Brush the cinnamon mixture over the surface of each pear half, ensuring they are well coated.
Bake Pears: Transfer the baking dish to the preheated oven and bake for 25-30 minutes, or until the pears are tender and caramelized.
Baste Pears (Optional): If desired, baste the pears with the juices halfway through baking to ensure they stay moist and flavorful.
Serve: Remove the baked pears from the oven and let them cool slightly. Serve warm, garnished with chopped nuts if desired.
Optional Serving Suggestion: Serve these cinnamon baked pears with a scoop of vanilla ice cream or a dollop of whipped cream for an extra special treat.
Enjoy: Enjoy these delicious cinnamon baked pears as a comforting and elegant dessert!

Notes:

- Choose pears that are ripe but still firm for the best texture after baking.
- Feel free to adjust the amount of honey or maple syrup based on the sweetness of your pears and your personal preference.
- Experiment with different spices such as cardamom or ginger for a unique flavor profile.
- Leftover baked pears can be stored in an airtight container in the refrigerator for a few days. Reheat gently in the microwave or oven before serving.

These cinnamon baked pears are a simple yet elegant dessert that highlights the natural sweetness of pears with warm spices. They are perfect for entertaining or enjoying as a cozy treat during cooler months. We hope you love making and savoring this delightful dessert!

Sugar-Free Pumpkin Pie

Ingredients:

For the Crust:

- 1 1/2 cups almond flour
- 1/4 cup coconut flour
- 1/4 cup melted coconut oil or butter
- 1 tablespoon powdered erythritol (or sweetener of choice)
- 1/2 teaspoon ground cinnamon
- Pinch of salt
- 1 large egg

For the Filling:

- 1 can (15 ounces) pumpkin puree (not pumpkin pie filling)
- 3 large eggs
- 1/2 cup heavy cream (or coconut cream for dairy-free)
- 1/2 cup powdered erythritol (or sweetener of choice)
- 1 teaspoon vanilla extract
- 1 teaspoon ground cinnamon
- 1/2 teaspoon ground ginger
- 1/4 teaspoon ground nutmeg
- 1/4 teaspoon ground cloves
- Pinch of salt

Instructions:

Preheat Oven: Preheat your oven to 350°F (175°C).
Make the Crust:
- In a mixing bowl, combine the almond flour, coconut flour, powdered erythritol, ground cinnamon, and a pinch of salt.
- Add the melted coconut oil or butter and the egg. Mix until a dough forms.
- Press the dough evenly into the bottom and up the sides of a 9-inch pie dish.
- Prick the bottom of the crust with a fork to prevent air bubbles.

Pre-Bake the Crust: Place the pie crust in the preheated oven and bake for 10-12 minutes, or until lightly golden. Remove from the oven and let it cool slightly while preparing the filling.

Make the Filling:

- In a large mixing bowl, whisk together the pumpkin puree, eggs, heavy cream (or coconut cream), powdered erythritol, vanilla extract, ground cinnamon, ground ginger, ground nutmeg, ground cloves, and a pinch of salt.
- Whisk until the mixture is smooth and well combined.

Pour into Crust: Pour the pumpkin filling into the pre-baked pie crust.

Bake the Pie: Place the pie in the oven and bake for 45-50 minutes, or until the center is set and no longer jiggly.

Cool and Chill: Remove the pie from the oven and let it cool completely at room temperature. Once cooled, refrigerate for at least 2 hours, or until chilled and set.

Serve: Slice and serve the sugar-free pumpkin pie chilled. Optionally, top with whipped cream or a dollop of coconut cream before serving.

Enjoy: Enjoy this delicious sugar-free pumpkin pie as a guilt-free dessert during the fall and holiday season!

Notes:

- Feel free to adjust the sweetness by adding more or less powdered erythritol according to your taste preferences.
- This pie can be made ahead of time and stored in the refrigerator for a few days before serving.
- Experiment with different spices or add a touch of orange zest for extra flavor variations.

This sugar-free pumpkin pie is rich, creamy, and full of warm spices, making it a perfect treat for those watching their sugar intake. It's a delightful dessert that everyone can enjoy, especially during festive occasions. We hope you have fun making and savoring this healthier version of a classic pumpkin pie!

Chocolate Chip Zucchini Muffins

Ingredients:

- 1 1/2 cups all-purpose flour
- 1/2 cup cocoa powder (unsweetened)
- 1 teaspoon baking powder
- 1/2 teaspoon baking soda
- 1/2 teaspoon salt
- 1/2 cup unsalted butter, melted
- 1/2 cup granulated sugar
- 1/2 cup packed brown sugar
- 2 large eggs
- 1 teaspoon vanilla extract
- 1 1/2 cups shredded zucchini (about 1 medium zucchini)
- 1/2 cup plain Greek yogurt (or sour cream)
- 1 cup chocolate chips (semi-sweet or dark)

Instructions:

Preheat Oven: Preheat your oven to 350°F (175°C). Line a muffin tin with paper liners or grease the muffin cups.
Prepare Dry Ingredients: In a medium bowl, whisk together the flour, cocoa powder, baking powder, baking soda, and salt. Set aside.
Mix Wet Ingredients: In a large mixing bowl, whisk together the melted butter, granulated sugar, and brown sugar until smooth. Add the eggs, one at a time, whisking well after each addition. Stir in the vanilla extract.
Add Zucchini and Yogurt: Stir in the shredded zucchini and Greek yogurt (or sour cream) until well combined.
Combine Dry and Wet Ingredients: Gradually add the dry ingredients to the wet ingredients, stirring until just combined. Be careful not to overmix.
Fold in Chocolate Chips: Gently fold in the chocolate chips until evenly distributed in the batter.
Fill Muffin Cups: Divide the batter evenly among the prepared muffin cups, filling each about 3/4 full.
Bake: Bake in the preheated oven for 18-20 minutes, or until a toothpick inserted into the center comes out clean or with a few moist crumbs (but no wet batter).
Cool and Serve: Allow the muffins to cool in the pan for 5 minutes, then transfer them to a wire rack to cool completely.

Enjoy: Serve these delicious chocolate chip zucchini muffins as a delightful snack or treat!

Notes:

- Make sure to squeeze excess moisture from the shredded zucchini before adding it to the batter to prevent the muffins from becoming too wet.
- You can customize these muffins by adding chopped nuts (such as walnuts or pecans) along with the chocolate chips.
- Store leftover muffins in an airtight container at room temperature for a few days, or freeze for longer storage. Reheat briefly in the microwave before serving if desired.

These chocolate chip zucchini muffins are moist, chocolaty, and perfect for using up garden-fresh zucchini. They make a great breakfast or snack option and are a wonderful way to sneak in some veggies. Enjoy baking and savoring these delicious muffins!

Blackberry Coconut Chia Popsicles

Ingredients:

- 1 cup fresh blackberries
- 1/2 cup canned coconut milk (full-fat)
- 1/2 cup unsweetened almond milk (or any milk of choice)
- 2 tablespoons chia seeds
- 2 tablespoons honey or maple syrup (adjust to taste)
- 1/2 teaspoon vanilla extract

Instructions:

Prepare Chia Gel: In a small bowl, combine the chia seeds with the almond milk. Stir well to mix, ensuring that the chia seeds are fully immersed in the liquid. Let the mixture sit for about 10-15 minutes, stirring occasionally, until it forms a gel-like consistency.

Blend Blackberries: In a blender or food processor, blend the fresh blackberries until smooth. You can strain the puree through a fine-mesh sieve to remove seeds if desired.

Mix Coconut Milk Mixture: In another bowl, whisk together the canned coconut milk, honey or maple syrup, and vanilla extract until smooth.

Combine Mixtures: Pour the blackberry puree, coconut milk mixture, and chia gel into a large mixing bowl. Gently fold together until fully combined.

Fill Popsicle Molds: Carefully pour the mixture into popsicle molds, leaving a little space at the top for expansion during freezing.

Insert Sticks: Place popsicle sticks into the molds.

Freeze: Transfer the popsicle molds to the freezer and freeze for at least 4-6 hours, or until the popsicles are completely frozen.

Unmold and Serve: Once frozen, remove the popsicles from the molds by running them under warm water for a few seconds. Gently pull the sticks to release the popsicles.

Enjoy: Serve and enjoy these refreshing blackberry coconut chia popsicles on a hot day!

Notes:

- Feel free to adjust the sweetness of the popsicles by adding more or less honey or maple syrup according to your taste.
- You can substitute fresh blackberries with any other berries of your choice, such as raspberries or blueberries.
- For added texture, you can sprinkle shredded coconut or chopped nuts into the popsicle molds before pouring the mixture.
- Store any leftover popsicles in the freezer in an airtight container or zip-top bag for future enjoyment.

These blackberry coconut chia popsicles are a delicious and healthy treat that's perfect for cooling off during warm weather. They are naturally sweetened and packed with fruity flavors and a hint of coconut. Enjoy making and sharing these delightful popsicles with family and friends!

Coconut Macaroons (sweetened with stevia)

Ingredients:

- 3 cups shredded coconut (unsweetened)
- 3 large egg whites
- 1/3 cup granulated stevia or powdered stevia blend (adjust to taste)
- 1 teaspoon vanilla extract
- Pinch of salt

Instructions:

Preheat Oven: Preheat your oven to 325°F (160°C). Line a baking sheet with parchment paper or a silicone baking mat.

Prepare Coconut Mixture: In a mixing bowl, combine the shredded coconut, granulated stevia (or powdered stevia blend), vanilla extract, and a pinch of salt. Mix well to combine.

Whip Egg Whites: In a separate bowl, use an electric mixer or stand mixer to beat the egg whites until stiff peaks form.

Combine Egg Whites with Coconut Mixture: Gently fold the whipped egg whites into the coconut mixture until fully incorporated. Be careful not to deflate the egg whites.

Shape Macaroons: Use a spoon or cookie scoop to portion the coconut mixture into mounds on the prepared baking sheet, about 1-2 tablespoons each. You can also use your hands to shape them into compact mounds.

Bake: Place the baking sheet in the preheated oven and bake for 20-25 minutes, or until the coconut macaroons are lightly golden on the outside.

Cool: Remove the baking sheet from the oven and let the coconut macaroons cool completely on the baking sheet.

Serve or Store: Once cooled, transfer the coconut macaroons to a serving plate or storage container. Enjoy them as a delicious low-sugar treat!

Notes:

- Adjust the sweetness to your taste by adding more or less granulated stevia.
- Make sure to use unsweetened shredded coconut to control the sweetness of the macaroons.

- You can drizzle melted sugar-free chocolate over the cooled macaroons for an extra special touch.
- Store leftover coconut macaroons in an airtight container at room temperature for a few days, or in the refrigerator for longer freshness.

These coconut macaroons sweetened with stevia are a delightful and guilt-free dessert option for those looking to reduce sugar intake. They are light, chewy, and packed with coconut flavor. Enjoy making and savoring these delicious treats!

Mango Coconut Rice Pudding

Ingredients:

- 1 cup jasmine rice (or any medium-grain rice)
- 2 cups water
- 1 can (13.5 oz) full-fat coconut milk
- 1/4 cup granulated sugar (or sweetener of choice)
- 1/2 teaspoon vanilla extract
- 1 ripe mango, peeled and diced
- Optional toppings: Toasted coconut flakes, chopped nuts, additional diced mango

Instructions:

Cook Rice: Rinse the jasmine rice under cold water until the water runs clear. In a medium saucepan, combine the rinsed rice and water. Bring to a boil over high heat, then reduce the heat to low, cover, and simmer for about 15-20 minutes, or until the rice is tender and the water is absorbed.
Prepare Coconut Milk Mixture: In another saucepan, combine the coconut milk and granulated sugar (or sweetener of choice) over medium heat. Stir until the sugar is dissolved and the mixture is smooth. Remove from heat and stir in the vanilla extract.
Combine Rice and Coconut Milk Mixture: Once the rice is cooked, pour the coconut milk mixture over the cooked rice. Stir well to combine.
Add Diced Mango: Gently fold in the diced mango into the rice pudding mixture.
Chill: Allow the mango coconut rice pudding to cool slightly, then transfer it to the refrigerator to chill for at least 1-2 hours, or until cold and set.
Serve: Divide the mango coconut rice pudding into serving bowls. Top with toasted coconut flakes, chopped nuts, or additional diced mango if desired.
Enjoy: Serve and enjoy this delicious mango coconut rice pudding as a refreshing and tropical dessert!

Notes:

- Adjust the sweetness of the rice pudding by adding more or less sugar according to your taste preference.
- Feel free to use other types of rice such as basmati or arborio rice for a different texture.

- You can substitute fresh mango with thawed frozen mango chunks if fresh mango is not available.
- For a creamier texture, you can stir in additional coconut milk or cream before chilling.
- Store any leftover mango coconut rice pudding in an airtight container in the refrigerator for up to 3-4 days.

This mango coconut rice pudding is a delightful and exotic dessert that combines the creaminess of coconut milk with the sweetness of ripe mangoes. It's perfect for enjoying during warm weather or as a special treat any time of the year. Enjoy making and savoring this tropical rice pudding!

Sugar-Free Lemon Bars

Ingredients:

For the Crust:

- 1 cup almond flour
- 1/4 cup coconut flour
- 1/4 cup granulated erythritol or sweetener of choice
- 1/4 teaspoon salt
- 1/4 cup melted coconut oil or butter
- 1 large egg

For the Lemon Filling:

- 4 large eggs
- Zest of 2 lemons
- 1 cup fresh lemon juice (from about 4-5 lemons)
- 1/2 cup granulated erythritol or sweetener of choice
- 1/4 cup coconut flour
- 1/4 teaspoon baking powder
- Powdered erythritol, for dusting (optional)

Instructions:

Preheat Oven: Preheat your oven to 350°F (175°C) and line an 8x8-inch baking dish with parchment paper.

Make the Crust:
- In a mixing bowl, combine almond flour, coconut flour, granulated erythritol, and salt.
- Add melted coconut oil or butter and egg to the dry ingredients. Mix until well combined and a dough forms.
- Press the dough evenly into the bottom of the prepared baking dish.

Bake the Crust: Place the crust in the preheated oven and bake for 12-15 minutes, or until golden brown around the edges. Remove from the oven and let it cool slightly.

Prepare the Lemon Filling:
- In a large bowl, whisk together eggs, lemon zest, lemon juice, and granulated erythritol until smooth.

- Add coconut flour and baking powder to the lemon mixture, whisking until well combined and no lumps remain.

Pour over Crust: Pour the lemon filling over the partially baked crust, spreading it out evenly.

Bake Again: Return the baking dish to the oven and bake for another 20-25 minutes, or until the filling is set and the edges are slightly golden.

Cool and Chill: Remove the lemon bars from the oven and let them cool completely in the baking dish. Transfer to the refrigerator and chill for at least 2 hours to set.

Slice and Serve: Once chilled, lift the parchment paper to remove the lemon bars from the dish. Dust with powdered erythritol if desired, then slice into squares.

Enjoy: Serve these delicious sugar-free lemon bars chilled and enjoy the refreshing lemony flavor!

Notes:

- Adjust the sweetness to your taste by adding more or less granulated erythritol.
- For a smoother texture, you can strain the lemon filling mixture before pouring it over the crust.
- Store leftover lemon bars in an airtight container in the refrigerator for up to 4-5 days.
- These bars can also be frozen for longer storage. Wrap them individually in plastic wrap and place in a freezer-safe container.

These sugar-free lemon bars are a delightful and tangy dessert option for those looking to enjoy a classic treat without the added sugar. They are perfect for special occasions or as a refreshing snack. Enjoy making and savoring these guilt-free lemon bars!

Avocado Lime Ice Cream

Ingredients:

- 2 ripe avocados, peeled and pitted
- 1 can (14 ounces) sweetened condensed milk
- 1/2 cup fresh lime juice (about 4-5 limes)
- Zest of 1 lime
- 1 cup heavy cream
- Green food coloring (optional, for a more vibrant green color)

Instructions:

Prepare Avocados: In a blender or food processor, combine the peeled and pitted avocados, sweetened condensed milk, fresh lime juice, and lime zest. Blend until smooth and creamy.
Chill Mixture: Transfer the avocado mixture into a mixing bowl. Cover with plastic wrap directly touching the surface of the mixture to prevent browning. Refrigerate for at least 1 hour to chill.
Whip Heavy Cream: In a separate bowl, whip the heavy cream until stiff peaks form.
Combine Mixtures: Gently fold the whipped cream into the chilled avocado mixture until well combined. Add green food coloring if desired for a vibrant green color.
Freeze: Transfer the mixture into a freezer-safe container or loaf pan. Cover with plastic wrap or a lid.
Chill in Freezer: Freeze the avocado lime ice cream mixture for at least 4-6 hours or until firm.
Serve: Scoop the avocado lime ice cream into bowls or cones. Garnish with additional lime zest or slices if desired.
Enjoy: Serve and enjoy this creamy and refreshing avocado lime ice cream!

Notes:

- Make sure to use ripe avocados for the best flavor and texture.
- Adjust the sweetness by adding more or less sweetened condensed milk based on your preference.
- For a dairy-free version, you can use coconut cream instead of heavy cream.

- Experiment with adding other mix-ins like chopped pistachios or white chocolate chips for added texture and flavor.

This avocado lime ice cream is a unique and delicious dessert that combines the creamy richness of avocado with the tangy zest of lime. It's perfect for cooling off on a hot day or as a refreshing treat any time of the year. Enjoy making and savoring this homemade ice cream!

Peanut Butter Banana "Nice" Cream

Ingredients:

- 3 ripe bananas, peeled, sliced, and frozen
- 1/4 cup creamy peanut butter (unsweetened)
- 1-2 tablespoons unsweetened almond milk (or any milk of choice), if needed
- Optional toppings: Chopped peanuts, chocolate chips, sliced bananas

Instructions:

Prepare Frozen Bananas: Slice ripe bananas into coins and place them in a single layer on a parchment-lined baking sheet. Freeze for at least 2-3 hours or until solid.
Blend Ingredients: In a food processor or high-speed blender, add the frozen banana slices and creamy peanut butter. Blend until smooth and creamy. If needed, add a tablespoon or two of almond milk to help with blending.
Scrape Down Sides: Stop blending occasionally to scrape down the sides of the food processor or blender to ensure even blending.
Adjust Consistency: Add more almond milk if needed to achieve a creamy ice cream-like consistency. Be cautious not to add too much liquid, as you want the nice cream to be thick and creamy.
Serve: Once blended to your desired consistency, scoop the peanut butter banana nice cream into bowls.
Add Toppings: Garnish with chopped peanuts, chocolate chips, or additional sliced bananas as desired.
Enjoy Immediately: Serve and enjoy this delicious and guilt-free peanut butter banana "nice" cream immediately!

Notes:

- Make sure to use ripe bananas for natural sweetness and the best texture.
- Customize the flavor by adding a splash of vanilla extract or a sprinkle of cinnamon to the nice cream mixture.
- Feel free to substitute peanut butter with almond butter or any other nut butter of your choice.

- This nice cream is best enjoyed fresh but can be stored in an airtight container in the freezer for later consumption. Allow it to thaw slightly before serving if frozen solid.

This peanut butter banana "nice" cream is a healthy and satisfying alternative to traditional ice cream, and it's easy to make with just a few simple ingredients. Enjoy this creamy and delicious treat as a guilt-free dessert or snack!

Blueberry Almond Flour Coffee Cake

Ingredients:

For the Cake:

- 2 cups almond flour
- 1/4 cup coconut flour
- 1/2 teaspoon baking soda
- 1/4 teaspoon salt
- 1/2 cup unsalted butter, softened
- 1/2 cup granulated erythritol (or sweetener of choice)
- 3 large eggs
- 1/4 cup unsweetened almond milk (or any milk of choice)
- 1 teaspoon vanilla extract
- 1 cup fresh or frozen blueberries (if using frozen, do not thaw)

For the Streusel Topping:

- 1/4 cup almond flour
- 2 tablespoons coconut flour
- 2 tablespoons granulated erythritol (or sweetener of choice)
- 2 tablespoons unsalted butter, melted
- 1/2 teaspoon ground cinnamon

Instructions:

Preheat Oven and Prepare Pan: Preheat your oven to 350°F (175°C). Grease an 8x8-inch baking dish or line it with parchment paper.
Make the Streusel Topping:
- In a small bowl, combine almond flour, coconut flour, granulated erythritol, melted butter, and ground cinnamon. Mix until crumbly. Set aside.

Prepare the Cake Batter:
- In a mixing bowl, whisk together almond flour, coconut flour, baking soda, and salt.
- In another large mixing bowl, cream together softened butter and granulated erythritol until smooth and fluffy.

- Add eggs, one at a time, mixing well after each addition.
- Stir in almond milk and vanilla extract.
- Gradually add the dry ingredients to the wet ingredients, mixing until well combined and smooth.

Add Blueberries: Gently fold in the blueberries into the cake batter.

Assemble the Cake:
- Pour the cake batter into the prepared baking dish, spreading it out evenly.
- Sprinkle the streusel topping over the top of the cake batter.

Bake: Place the baking dish in the preheated oven and bake for 30-35 minutes, or until the top is golden brown and a toothpick inserted into the center comes out clean.

Cool and Serve: Allow the blueberry almond flour coffee cake to cool in the pan for at least 15-20 minutes before slicing and serving.

Enjoy: Serve this delicious coffee cake warm or at room temperature. It's perfect for breakfast, brunch, or as a delightful dessert!

Notes:

- Make sure to use almond flour and coconut flour for the best texture in this gluten-free coffee cake.
- Adjust the sweetness by adding more or less granulated erythritol according to your taste preference.
- Feel free to substitute blueberries with other berries such as raspberries or blackberries.
- Store leftover coffee cake in an airtight container at room temperature for a couple of days, or refrigerate for longer freshness. Reheat briefly in the microwave before serving if desired.

This blueberry almond flour coffee cake is a wonderful gluten-free and low-carb treat that's perfect for enjoying with a cup of coffee or tea. It's moist, flavorful, and bursting with juicy blueberries. Enjoy baking and savoring this delightful coffee cake!

No-Bake Almond Butter Bars

Ingredients:

- 1 cup almond butter (creamy or crunchy)
- 1/4 cup coconut oil, melted
- 1/4 cup powdered erythritol (or sweetener of choice)
- 1 teaspoon vanilla extract
- 2 cups almond flour
- 1/4 teaspoon salt
- 1/2 cup sugar-free chocolate chips (optional, for topping)

Instructions:

Prepare the Base:
- In a large mixing bowl, combine almond butter, melted coconut oil, powdered erythritol, and vanilla extract. Mix until smooth and well combined.

Add Dry Ingredients:
- Add almond flour and salt to the almond butter mixture. Stir until a thick dough forms.

Press into Pan:
- Line an 8x8-inch baking dish with parchment paper for easy removal.
- Transfer the almond butter mixture into the prepared baking dish.
- Use your hands or a spatula to evenly press the mixture into the bottom of the dish.

Optional Chocolate Topping:
- If desired, melt the sugar-free chocolate chips in the microwave or using a double boiler.
- Drizzle the melted chocolate over the top of the almond butter bars.

Chill:
- Place the baking dish in the refrigerator for at least 1-2 hours to allow the bars to firm up.

Slice and Serve:
- Once chilled and firm, remove the bars from the baking dish using the parchment paper.
- Use a sharp knife to slice the bars into squares or rectangles.

Enjoy:

- Serve and enjoy these delicious no-bake almond butter bars as a healthy snack or dessert!

Notes:

- Store leftover almond butter bars in an airtight container in the refrigerator for up to one week.
- Feel free to customize these bars by adding chopped nuts, seeds, or dried fruits to the almond butter mixture.
- You can substitute almond flour with other nut or seed flours if needed.
- Adjust the sweetness by adding more or less powdered erythritol according to your taste preference.

These no-bake almond butter bars are easy to make and require minimal effort. They are perfect for satisfying sweet cravings without the need for baking. Enjoy making and savoring these delicious homemade bars!

Raspberry Coconut Milk Rice Pudding

Ingredients:

- 1 cup jasmine rice (or any medium-grain rice)
- 1 can (13.5 oz) coconut milk (full-fat)
- 2 cups water
- 1/4 cup granulated erythritol (or sweetener of choice), adjust to taste
- 1/2 teaspoon vanilla extract
- 1 cup fresh raspberries (or frozen raspberries, thawed)

Instructions:

Rinse and Cook Rice:
- Rinse the jasmine rice under cold water until the water runs clear.
- In a medium saucepan, combine the rinsed rice, coconut milk, and water. Bring to a boil over medium-high heat.
- Reduce the heat to low, cover, and simmer for about 15-20 minutes, or until the rice is tender and most of the liquid is absorbed.

Sweeten and Flavor:
- Stir in the granulated erythritol (or sweetener of choice) and vanilla extract into the cooked rice. Adjust sweetness according to your taste.

Add Raspberries:
- Gently fold in the fresh raspberries into the rice pudding mixture. If using frozen raspberries, make sure they are thawed and well-drained before adding.

Simmer and Serve:
- Cook the rice pudding mixture for an additional 5 minutes over low heat, stirring occasionally, until the raspberries are softened and the pudding reaches your desired consistency.
- Remove from heat and let it cool slightly.

Serve Warm or Chilled:
- Serve the raspberry coconut milk rice pudding warm or chilled, depending on your preference.

Optional Garnish:
- Garnish with extra fresh raspberries on top before serving for an added burst of flavor and visual appeal.

Enjoy:

- Enjoy this delightful raspberry coconut milk rice pudding as a comforting dessert or sweet breakfast treat!

Notes:

- Adjust the sweetness of the rice pudding by adding more or less sweetener according to your preference.
- Feel free to substitute the jasmine rice with another type of rice such as arborio or basmati for a different texture.
- You can also add a sprinkle of cinnamon or a dash of lemon zest for extra flavor.
- Store any leftover rice pudding in an airtight container in the refrigerator for up to 3-4 days. Reheat briefly before serving if desired.

This raspberry coconut milk rice pudding is a creamy and flavorful dessert that combines the sweetness of raspberries with the richness of coconut milk. It's perfect for enjoying as a cozy treat any time of the day. Enjoy making and savoring this delicious rice pudding!

Chocolate Covered Strawberries (using sugar-free chocolate)

Ingredients:

- 1 pound fresh strawberries, washed and dried thoroughly
- 6 ounces sugar-free dark chocolate (chips or chopped bar)
- 1 tablespoon coconut oil or vegetable shortening (optional, for thinning the chocolate)
- Optional toppings: Chopped nuts, shredded coconut, sea salt

Instructions:

Prepare Strawberries:
- Wash and thoroughly dry the strawberries using paper towels. Make sure they are completely dry to prevent the chocolate from seizing.

Melt Sugar-Free Chocolate:
- In a microwave-safe bowl or using a double boiler, melt the sugar-free dark chocolate until smooth. If using a microwave, heat the chocolate in 30-second intervals, stirring between each interval until melted. Be careful not to overheat the chocolate.

Thin Chocolate (Optional):
- If the melted chocolate is too thick for dipping, stir in 1 tablespoon of coconut oil or vegetable shortening to thin it out. This will make the chocolate smoother and easier to coat the strawberries.

Dip Strawberries:
- Hold each strawberry by the stem and dip it into the melted chocolate, swirling to coat about two-thirds of the berry. Allow any excess chocolate to drip back into the bowl.

Place on Parchment Paper:
- Place each chocolate-covered strawberry onto a parchment-lined baking sheet. This will prevent them from sticking and make cleanup easier.

Add Optional Toppings:
- While the chocolate is still wet, sprinkle optional toppings such as chopped nuts, shredded coconut, or a pinch of sea salt over the strawberries.

Chill and Set:
- Once all strawberries are dipped and decorated, place the baking sheet in the refrigerator for about 30 minutes, or until the chocolate is set and firm.

Serve and Enjoy:
- Once the chocolate has set, remove the chocolate-covered strawberries from the refrigerator and arrange them on a serving platter.
- Serve immediately and enjoy these delicious sugar-free chocolate covered strawberries as a decadent and guilt-free treat!

Notes:

- Use sugar-free dark chocolate that is specifically formulated for melting and coating, as some brands of sugar-free chocolate may not behave the same way as regular chocolate.
- Customize your chocolate covered strawberries by experimenting with different toppings such as crushed nuts, unsweetened coconut flakes, or a sprinkle of sea salt for a gourmet touch.
- Store any leftover chocolate covered strawberries in an airtight container in the refrigerator for up to 2-3 days. Enjoy them chilled for the best taste and texture.

These sugar-free chocolate covered strawberries are a delightful and healthier alternative to traditional chocolate-covered treats. They are perfect for special occasions, parties, or as a romantic dessert. Enjoy making and indulging in these delicious treats!

Vania Chia Seed Pudding

Ingredients:

- 1/4 cup chia seeds
- 1 cup unsweetened almond milk (or any milk of your choice)
- 1 tablespoon maple syrup or sweetener of choice (adjust to taste)
- 1/2 teaspoon vanilla extract
- Optional toppings: Fresh berries, sliced bananas, chopped nuts, coconut flakes

Instructions:

Combine Chia Seeds and Liquid:
- In a mixing bowl or jar, combine chia seeds, unsweetened almond milk, maple syrup (or sweetener), and vanilla extract. Stir well to combine.

Mix Thoroughly:
- Stir the mixture thoroughly to ensure the chia seeds are evenly distributed and not clumping together.

Refrigerate and Rest:
- Cover the bowl or jar and refrigerate for at least 2 hours, or ideally overnight. This allows the chia seeds to absorb the liquid and thicken into a pudding-like consistency.

Stir Again (Optional):
- After the initial refrigeration period, give the chia seed mixture another stir to break up any clumps and ensure an even texture.

Serve and Enjoy:
- Divide the chilled chia seed pudding into serving bowls or glasses.
- Top with your favorite toppings such as fresh berries, sliced bananas, chopped nuts, or coconut flakes.

Storage:
- Store any leftover chia seed pudding in an airtight container in the refrigerator for up to 3-4 days. Stir before serving if needed.

Notes:

- Customize your vanilla chia seed pudding by adjusting the sweetness and flavorings to your preference. You can use honey, agave syrup, or any preferred sweetener instead of maple syrup.
- For a richer pudding, use canned coconut milk instead of almond milk.

- Experiment with different toppings to create delicious flavor combinations. Consider adding cinnamon, cocoa powder, or flavored extracts for variety.
- Chia seed pudding can be enjoyed as a healthy breakfast, snack, or dessert. It's packed with fiber, omega-3 fatty acids, and nutrients.

This vanilla chia seed pudding is a simple and nutritious treat that can be enjoyed any time of day. It's versatile, customizable, and a great way to incorporate chia seeds into your diet. Enjoy making and savoring this delicious pudding!

Sugar-Free Oatmeal Raisin Cookies

Ingredients:

- 1 cup old-fashioned rolled oats
- 3/4 cup almond flour
- 1/2 teaspoon baking soda
- 1/2 teaspoon ground cinnamon
- 1/4 teaspoon salt
- 1/4 cup unsalted butter, melted
- 1/4 cup sugar-free sweetener (erythritol, stevia, monk fruit, etc.)
- 1 large egg
- 1 teaspoon vanilla extract
- 1/2 cup raisins (unsweetened or sugar-free, if preferred)

Instructions:

Preheat Oven: Preheat your oven to 350°F (175°C). Line a baking sheet with parchment paper or lightly grease it.

Mix Dry Ingredients: In a mixing bowl, combine the rolled oats, almond flour, baking soda, ground cinnamon, and salt. Mix well and set aside.

Prepare Wet Ingredients: In another bowl, whisk together the melted butter and sugar-free sweetener until smooth. Add the egg and vanilla extract, and whisk until well combined.

Combine Wet and Dry Ingredients: Pour the wet ingredients into the bowl of dry ingredients. Mix until everything is well incorporated and forms a cookie dough. Fold in the raisins until evenly distributed.

Form Cookies: Use a spoon or cookie scoop to portion out the cookie dough onto the prepared baking sheet, leaving space between each cookie for spreading.

Bake Cookies: Place the baking sheet in the preheated oven and bake for 12-15 minutes, or until the cookies are golden brown around the edges.

Cool and Enjoy: Allow the cookies to cool on the baking sheet for a few minutes, then transfer them to a wire rack to cool completely.

Store: Store the sugar-free oatmeal raisin cookies in an airtight container at room temperature for up to 5 days. They can also be frozen for longer storage.

Notes:

- Feel free to adjust the amount of sweetener to your taste preference. Taste the cookie dough before baking and add more sweetener if desired.
- You can substitute the almond flour with other low-carb flour alternatives like coconut flour or a gluten-free flour blend.
- For added flavor, consider adding a dash of nutmeg or cloves to the cookie dough.
- If you prefer softer cookies, slightly underbake them by reducing the baking time by a couple of minutes.

These sugar-free oatmeal raisin cookies are a healthier alternative to traditional cookies, perfect for anyone looking to reduce their sugar intake. Enjoy these delicious treats as a snack or dessert without the guilt!

Pumpkin Spice Energy Balls

Ingredients:

- 1 cup rolled oats
- 1/2 cup pumpkin puree (canned or homemade)
- 1/4 cup almond butter (or any nut or seed butter of choice)
- 1/4 cup maple syrup or honey (adjust to taste)
- 1 teaspoon pumpkin pie spice (or a combination of cinnamon, nutmeg, and cloves)
- 1/2 teaspoon vanilla extract
- Pinch of salt
- Optional: Chopped nuts, dried cranberries, or mini chocolate chips for mixing in or rolling

Instructions:

Mix Ingredients: In a mixing bowl, combine rolled oats, pumpkin puree, almond butter, maple syrup (or honey), pumpkin pie spice, vanilla extract, and a pinch of salt. Stir until well combined.
Add Mix-Ins (Optional): If desired, fold in chopped nuts, dried cranberries, or mini chocolate chips for added texture and flavor.
Chill Mixture: Place the mixture in the refrigerator for about 30 minutes to firm up slightly. This will make it easier to roll into balls.
Roll into Balls: Once chilled, take tablespoon-sized portions of the mixture and roll them into balls using your hands. If the mixture is too sticky, lightly dampen your hands with water.
Optional Coating: Roll the energy balls in additional rolled oats, shredded coconut, or cocoa powder for an extra layer of flavor and texture.
Chill and Store: Place the pumpkin spice energy balls in an airtight container and store them in the refrigerator for up to one week.
Enjoy: Grab a pumpkin spice energy ball as a quick and healthy snack or treat throughout the day!

Notes:

- Adjust the sweetness of the energy balls by adding more or less maple syrup or honey to suit your taste preference.

- Feel free to customize the energy balls by adding your favorite mix-ins such as chopped nuts, seeds, or dried fruits.
- Make sure to use pure pumpkin puree (not pumpkin pie filling) for the best flavor and texture.
- These energy balls are portable and perfect for on-the-go snacking, pre or post-workout fuel, or a healthy treat during fall.

These pumpkin spice energy balls are a delicious and nutritious snack packed with seasonal flavors. They are easy to make, require no baking, and can be enjoyed by the whole family. Enjoy making and savoring these delightful energy balls!

Watermelon Sorbet

Ingredients:

- 4 cups seedless watermelon, diced (about 1 small watermelon)
- 1/4 cup fresh lime juice (about 2-3 limes)
- 1/4 cup honey or agave syrup (adjust to taste)
- Optional: Mint leaves, for garnish

Instructions:

Prepare Watermelon:
- Cut the seedless watermelon into small chunks, removing any seeds and rind.

Blend Ingredients:
- In a blender or food processor, combine the diced watermelon, fresh lime juice, and honey (or agave syrup). Blend until smooth and well combined.

Strain (Optional):
- If you prefer a smoother texture, strain the watermelon mixture through a fine-mesh sieve to remove any pulp or seeds.

Chill Mixture:
- Transfer the blended watermelon mixture into a shallow dish or bowl. Cover and place it in the refrigerator to chill for about 1-2 hours, or until cold.

Churn in Ice Cream Maker (Optional):
- If you have an ice cream maker, pour the chilled watermelon mixture into the machine and churn according to the manufacturer's instructions until it reaches a sorbet-like consistency.

Freeze Without Ice Cream Maker:
- If you don't have an ice cream maker, transfer the chilled watermelon mixture into a shallow dish or pan. Place it in the freezer.
- Every 30 minutes, use a fork to scrape and stir the mixture to break up any ice crystals. Repeat this process until the sorbet is frozen and has a smooth texture, about 2-3 hours.

Serve and Enjoy:
- Once the watermelon sorbet reaches your desired consistency, scoop it into bowls or glasses.
- Garnish with fresh mint leaves if desired.

- Serve immediately and enjoy this refreshing watermelon sorbet!

Notes:

- Adjust the sweetness of the sorbet by adding more or less honey or agave syrup based on the natural sweetness of your watermelon.
- For a fun twist, try adding a splash of vodka or rum to the watermelon mixture before freezing to prevent it from becoming too icy.
- Store any leftover watermelon sorbet in an airtight container in the freezer. Let it sit at room temperature for a few minutes before scooping if it becomes too hard.

This watermelon sorbet is a light and refreshing dessert perfect for hot summer days.

It's easy to make and a great way to use up fresh watermelon. Enjoy making and savoring this homemade sorbet!

Orange Creamsicles (made with unsweetened coconut milk)

Ingredients:

- 1 cup fresh orange juice (about 3-4 large oranges)
- 1 cup unsweetened coconut milk (canned or carton)
- 2-3 tablespoons honey or maple syrup (adjust to taste)
- 1 teaspoon vanilla extract
- Zest of 1 orange (optional, for extra flavor)

Instructions:

Prepare Orange Juice:
- Squeeze enough fresh oranges to yield 1 cup of orange juice. Remove any pulp or seeds.

Mix Ingredients:
- In a mixing bowl or blender, combine the fresh orange juice, unsweetened coconut milk, honey (or maple syrup), vanilla extract, and orange zest (if using). Stir or blend until well combined.

Taste and Adjust:
- Taste the mixture and adjust sweetness by adding more honey or maple syrup if desired.

Pour into Molds:
- Pour the orange coconut mixture into popsicle molds, leaving a little space at the top for expansion.

Insert Sticks:
- Insert popsicle sticks into each mold. If your molds don't have built-in sticks, you can cover the molds with foil and insert sticks through the foil.

Freeze:
- Place the molds in the freezer and let them freeze for at least 4-6 hours, or until solid.

Unmold and Serve:
- Once fully frozen, remove the orange creamsicles from the molds.
- To release the popsicles, briefly run the molds under warm water or dip them into a bowl of warm water.

Enjoy:
- Serve and enjoy these refreshing homemade orange creamsicles on a hot day!

Notes:

- If you prefer a creamier texture, you can use full-fat canned coconut milk instead of carton coconut milk.
- For a more intense orange flavor, add extra orange zest to the mixture.
- Feel free to experiment with other citrus fruits like lemon or lime to create different flavored creamsicles.
- Store any leftover orange creamsicles in an airtight container in the freezer for up to 1-2 weeks.

These orange creamsicles made with unsweetened coconut milk are a delightful and healthier alternative to store-bought treats. They are easy to make and perfect for cooling off during the summer months. Enjoy making and savoring these homemade creamsicles!

Almond Butter Chocolate Cups

Ingredients:

- 1/2 cup creamy almond butter
- 2 tablespoons coconut oil, divided
- 2 tablespoons powdered erythritol or sweetener of choice
- 1/2 teaspoon vanilla extract
- Pinch of salt
- 4 ounces sugar-free dark chocolate (chips or chopped bar)

Instructions:

Prepare Almond Butter Filling:
- In a bowl, combine almond butter, 1 tablespoon of coconut oil, powdered erythritol (or sweetener), vanilla extract, and a pinch of salt. Mix until smooth and well combined. Adjust sweetness to taste.

Melt Chocolate:
- In a microwave-safe bowl or using a double boiler, melt the sugar-free dark chocolate along with the remaining 1 tablespoon of coconut oil until smooth and melted.

Assemble Chocolate Cups:
- Line a mini muffin tin with mini paper or silicone liners.
- Spoon a small amount of melted chocolate into the bottom of each liner, just enough to cover the bottom.

Add Almond Butter Filling:
- Place a small spoonful of almond butter filling on top of the melted chocolate in each liner, pressing down slightly to flatten.

Top with Remaining Chocolate:
- Pour the remaining melted chocolate over the almond butter filling in each liner, covering completely and smoothing the top with a spoon.

Chill and Set:
- Place the muffin tin in the refrigerator for about 1-2 hours, or until the almond butter chocolate cups are firm and set.

Serve and Enjoy:
- Once set, remove the almond butter chocolate cups from the muffin tin and peel off the liners.
- Serve and enjoy these delicious homemade treats!

Notes:

- Feel free to use any nut butter of your choice (such as peanut butter or cashew butter) instead of almond butter.
- Adjust the sweetness by adding more or less powdered erythritol or sweetener according to your taste preference.
- Store the almond butter chocolate cups in an airtight container in the refrigerator for up to one week. Enjoy them chilled for the best taste and texture.

These almond butter chocolate cups are a delightful and satisfying treat that combines creamy almond butter with rich sugar-free dark chocolate. They are perfect for satisfying sweet cravings while being low in carbs and sugar. Enjoy making and indulging in these homemade chocolate cups!

Sugar-Free Lemon Loaf Cake

Ingredients:

- 1 1/2 cups almond flour
- 1/4 cup coconut flour
- 1 teaspoon baking powder
- 1/4 teaspoon salt
- 1/2 cup unsalted butter, melted
- 1/2 cup granulated erythritol (or sweetener of choice)
- 3 large eggs
- Zest of 2 lemons
- 1/4 cup fresh lemon juice
- 1 teaspoon vanilla extract
- Optional: 1/4 cup unsweetened almond milk (if needed for batter consistency)

Lemon Glaze (Optional):

- 1/4 cup powdered erythritol (or sweetener of choice)
- 2-3 tablespoons fresh lemon juice

Instructions:

Preheat Oven: Preheat your oven to 350°F (175°C). Grease a loaf pan or line it with parchment paper.

Mix Dry Ingredients: In a bowl, whisk together almond flour, coconut flour, baking powder, and salt until well combined. Set aside.

Prepare Wet Ingredients: In a separate bowl, mix melted butter and granulated erythritol until smooth. Add eggs one at a time, mixing well after each addition. Stir in lemon zest, lemon juice, and vanilla extract.

Combine Wet and Dry Ingredients: Gradually add the dry flour mixture into the wet ingredients, stirring until a thick batter forms. If the batter is too thick, add unsweetened almond milk a tablespoon at a time until desired consistency is reached.

Bake: Pour the batter into the prepared loaf pan and spread it out evenly. Bake in the preheated oven for 40-45 minutes, or until a toothpick inserted into the center comes out clean.

Cool: Allow the lemon loaf cake to cool in the pan for 10-15 minutes, then transfer it to a wire rack to cool completely.

Prepare Lemon Glaze (Optional): In a small bowl, whisk together powdered erythritol and fresh lemon juice until smooth and pourable.

Glaze the Cake: Once the cake is completely cooled, drizzle the lemon glaze over the top. Allow the glaze to set before slicing and serving.

Serve and Enjoy: Slice the sugar-free lemon loaf cake into pieces and serve. Enjoy with a cup of tea or coffee!

Notes:

- Adjust sweetness to taste by adding more or less granulated erythritol in the cake batter.
- You can substitute the almond flour with another nut flour or gluten-free flour blend if needed.
- The lemon glaze is optional but adds extra flavor and sweetness to the cake.
- Store any leftover lemon loaf cake in an airtight container in the refrigerator for up to 4-5 days. Bring to room temperature before serving.

This sugar-free lemon loaf cake is moist, flavorful, and perfect for citrus lovers looking for a low-carb dessert option. Enjoy baking and savoring this delightful treat!

Berry Crumble Bars (using sugar-free sweetener)

Ingredients:

For the Berry Filling:

- 2 cups mixed berries (such as raspberries, blueberries, blackberries)
- 2 tablespoons lemon juice
- 2 tablespoons powdered erythritol (or sweetener of choice)
- 1 tablespoon arrowroot powder or cornstarch

For the Crumble Dough:

- 1 1/2 cups almond flour
- 1/4 cup coconut flour
- 1/3 cup powdered erythritol (or sweetener of choice)
- 1/4 teaspoon salt
- 1/2 cup unsalted butter, melted
- 1 teaspoon vanilla extract

Instructions:

Preheat Oven: Preheat your oven to 350°F (175°C). Grease or line an 8x8-inch baking dish with parchment paper.
Make the Berry Filling:
- In a bowl, combine the mixed berries, lemon juice, powdered erythritol, and arrowroot powder (or cornstarch). Toss gently to coat the berries evenly.

Prepare the Crumble Dough:
- In a separate bowl, mix together almond flour, coconut flour, powdered erythritol, and salt.
- Add melted butter and vanilla extract to the dry mixture. Stir until well combined and a crumbly dough forms.

Assemble the Bars:
- Press about two-thirds of the crumble dough evenly into the bottom of the prepared baking dish, forming the base of the bars.
- Spread the berry filling over the dough layer, distributing it evenly.

Add Crumble Topping:

- Sprinkle the remaining crumble dough evenly over the berry filling, covering it as much as possible.

Bake:
- Bake in the preheated oven for 30-35 minutes, or until the top is golden brown and the berry filling is bubbling around the edges.

Cool and Slice:
- Allow the berry crumble bars to cool completely in the baking dish before slicing into bars.

Serve and Enjoy:
- Once cooled and sliced, serve these delicious sugar-free berry crumble bars as a tasty treat or dessert option.

Notes:

- Feel free to use any combination of berries you prefer or have on hand.
- Adjust the sweetness of the filling by adding more or less powdered erythritol based on your taste preference.
- These bars can be stored in an airtight container in the refrigerator for up to 4-5 days. Enjoy them chilled or at room temperature.

These sugar-free berry crumble bars are a delightful way to enjoy the sweetness of berries without added sugar. They make a perfect dessert or snack, and the almond flour crust adds a nice texture to complement the fruity filling. Enjoy making and savoring these delicious bars!

Chocolate Chip Chickpea Blondies

Ingredients:

- 1 can (15 oz) chickpeas (garbanzo beans), drained and rinsed
- 1/2 cup almond butter (or any nut butter of choice)
- 1/3 cup maple syrup or honey
- 2 teaspoons vanilla extract
- 1/2 teaspoon baking powder
- 1/4 teaspoon baking soda
- 1/4 teaspoon salt
- 1/2 cup sugar-free chocolate chips (or regular chocolate chips if preferred)

Instructions:

Preheat Oven: Preheat your oven to 350°F (175°C). Grease or line an 8x8-inch baking pan with parchment paper.
Blend Chickpeas: In a food processor or high-speed blender, combine the drained and rinsed chickpeas, almond butter, maple syrup (or honey), vanilla extract, baking powder, baking soda, and salt. Blend until smooth and creamy, scraping down the sides as needed.
Stir in Chocolate Chips: Transfer the chickpea mixture to a mixing bowl. Stir in the sugar-free chocolate chips until evenly distributed.
Bake: Pour the batter into the prepared baking pan and spread it out evenly with a spatula.
Add Extra Chocolate Chips (Optional): Sprinkle additional chocolate chips on top of the batter if desired for extra chocolatey goodness.
Bake: Bake in the preheated oven for 20-25 minutes, or until the edges are golden brown and a toothpick inserted into the center comes out clean.
Cool and Slice: Allow the chickpea blondies to cool in the pan for at least 15-20 minutes before slicing into squares.
Serve and Enjoy: Serve these delicious chocolate chip chickpea blondies as a healthy dessert or snack option.

Notes:

- Ensure the chickpeas are well blended to achieve a smooth and creamy batter. You may need to scrape down the sides of the food processor or blender a few times.
- Feel free to customize the recipe by adding chopped nuts, dried fruits, or other mix-ins along with the chocolate chips.
- Store any leftover chickpea blondies in an airtight container in the refrigerator for up to 4-5 days. Enjoy them chilled or at room temperature.

These chocolate chip chickpea blondies are a nutritious and tasty treat packed with protein and fiber from the chickpeas. They are naturally sweetened and make a great guilt-free indulgence. Enjoy making and savoring these delightful blondies!

Matcha Coconut Bliss Balls

Ingredients:

- 1 cup shredded coconut (unsweetened)
- 1/2 cup almond flour
- 2 tablespoons coconut oil, melted
- 2 tablespoons honey or maple syrup
- 1 tablespoon matcha powder
- 1 teaspoon vanilla extract
- Pinch of salt

Optional Coating:

- Additional shredded coconut
- Matcha powder

Instructions:

Combine Ingredients: In a food processor, combine shredded coconut, almond flour, melted coconut oil, honey (or maple syrup), matcha powder, vanilla extract, and a pinch of salt. Pulse until the mixture comes together and forms a dough-like consistency.
Chill Mixture: Transfer the mixture to a bowl and refrigerate for about 15-20 minutes to firm up slightly, which will make it easier to roll into balls.
Roll into Balls: Remove the chilled mixture from the refrigerator. Take small portions and roll them into balls using your hands. The size of the balls is up to you, but aim for bite-sized portions.
Optional Coating: If desired, roll the bliss balls in additional shredded coconut or matcha powder for a decorative and flavorful coating.
Chill and Serve: Place the matcha coconut bliss balls in an airtight container and refrigerate for at least 30 minutes to firm up further before serving.
Enjoy: Serve and enjoy these delicious matcha coconut bliss balls as a healthy snack or dessert option.

Notes:

- Adjust the sweetness by adding more or less honey or maple syrup based on your preference.
- If the mixture is too dry and crumbly, add a bit more melted coconut oil or honey to help it stick together.
- Store the bliss balls in the refrigerator in an airtight container for up to one week. They can also be frozen for longer storage.

These matcha coconut bliss balls are a delightful combination of flavors and textures, with the earthy notes of matcha complementing the sweetness of coconut and honey. They make a great energizing snack and are perfect for satisfying your sweet cravings in a healthier way. Enjoy making and savoring these delicious bliss balls!

Peanut Butter Banana Ice Cream Sandwiches

Ingredients:

For the Banana Ice Cream:

- 4 ripe bananas, peeled, sliced, and frozen
- 2-3 tablespoons creamy peanut butter
- 1 teaspoon vanilla extract

For the Cookie "Buns":

- 1 cup almond flour
- 1/4 cup coconut flour
- 1/4 cup natural creamy peanut butter
- 1/4 cup maple syrup or honey
- 1/4 cup coconut oil, melted
- 1 teaspoon vanilla extract
- 1/4 teaspoon salt

Instructions:

Make Banana Ice Cream:
- In a food processor or high-speed blender, blend the frozen banana slices, creamy peanut butter, and vanilla extract until smooth and creamy. You may need to scrape down the sides occasionally. Transfer the banana ice cream mixture to a container and freeze for at least 2 hours to firm up.

Prepare Cookie "Buns":
- Preheat your oven to 350°F (175°C). Line a baking sheet with parchment paper.
- In a bowl, mix together almond flour, coconut flour, natural creamy peanut butter, maple syrup (or honey), melted coconut oil, vanilla extract, and salt until a dough forms.
- Divide the dough into 12 equal portions and roll each portion into a ball. Place the balls on the prepared baking sheet and flatten them slightly with your palm to form cookie shapes.

- Bake in the preheated oven for 10-12 minutes, or until the edges are golden brown. Remove from the oven and let the cookies cool completely.

Assemble Ice Cream Sandwiches:
- Once the cookies and banana ice cream are completely chilled, assemble the ice cream sandwiches.
- Take one cookie and spread a scoop of banana ice cream on top. Place another cookie on top to form a sandwich.
- Repeat with the remaining cookies and banana ice cream to make more sandwiches.

Freeze and Serve:
- Place the assembled ice cream sandwiches in the freezer for at least 1 hour to allow them to firm up.
- Serve and enjoy these delicious peanut butter banana ice cream sandwiches as a cool and satisfying treat!

Notes:

- Customize these ice cream sandwiches by adding chocolate chips or chopped nuts to the cookie dough.
- Store any leftover ice cream sandwiches in an airtight container in the freezer. Let them sit at room temperature for a few minutes before serving to soften slightly.
- Experiment with different nut butters or flavor variations for the banana ice cream and cookie "buns" to create unique combinations.

These peanut butter banana ice cream sandwiches are a delightful and healthier alternative to traditional ice cream treats. They are easy to make and perfect for satisfying sweet cravings with wholesome ingredients. Enjoy making and savoring these delicious homemade ice cream sandwiches!

Blueberry Almond Flour Scones

Ingredients:

- 2 cups almond flour
- 1/4 cup coconut flour
- 1/4 cup granulated erythritol (or sweetener of choice)
- 1 teaspoon baking powder
- 1/4 teaspoon salt
- 1/4 cup cold unsalted butter, cubed
- 1/4 cup unsweetened almond milk (or any milk of choice)
- 1 large egg
- 1 teaspoon vanilla extract
- 1/2 cup fresh or frozen blueberries

Optional Glaze:

- 1/4 cup powdered erythritol (or sweetener of choice)
- 1-2 tablespoons unsweetened almond milk (or any milk of choice)
- 1/4 teaspoon vanilla extract

Instructions:

Preheat Oven: Preheat your oven to 350°F (175°C). Line a baking sheet with parchment paper.
Mix Dry Ingredients: In a large bowl, whisk together almond flour, coconut flour, granulated erythritol, baking powder, and salt.
Cut in Butter: Using a pastry cutter or fork, cut the cold cubed butter into the dry ingredients until the mixture resembles coarse crumbs.
Combine Wet Ingredients: In a separate bowl, whisk together almond milk, egg, and vanilla extract.
Form Dough: Pour the wet ingredients into the dry ingredients and mix until just combined. Gently fold in the blueberries.
Shape Scones: Transfer the dough onto a parchment-lined surface. Pat the dough into a circle about 1-inch thick. Use a sharp knife to cut the circle into 8 equal wedges.
Bake Scones: Carefully transfer the wedges to the prepared baking sheet, spacing them apart. Bake for 18-22 minutes, or until the scones are golden brown and cooked through.

Optional Glaze (if desired):
- In a small bowl, whisk together powdered erythritol, almond milk, and vanilla extract to make the glaze.
- Drizzle the glaze over the cooled scones.

Serve and Enjoy: Allow the scones to cool slightly before serving. Enjoy these delicious blueberry almond flour scones with your favorite hot beverage!

Notes:

- Ensure your butter is cold when cutting it into the dry ingredients to achieve a flaky texture in the scones.
- If using frozen blueberries, you can toss them in a little coconut flour to prevent them from sinking to the bottom of the scones.
- Adjust the sweetness by adding more or less sweetener according to your taste preference.
- Store any leftover scones in an airtight container at room temperature for up to 2 days, or in the refrigerator for longer freshness.

These blueberry almond flour scones are a wonderful gluten-free and low-carb treat perfect for breakfast or afternoon tea. They are tender, lightly sweetened, and bursting with juicy blueberries. Enjoy making and savoring these delightful scones!

No-Bake Coconut Cream Pie

Ingredients:

For the Crust:

- 1 1/2 cups shredded coconut (unsweetened)
- 1/4 cup almond flour
- 1/4 cup coconut oil, melted
- 2 tablespoons powdered erythritol (or sweetener of choice)
- Pinch of salt

For the Coconut Cream Filling:

- 1 can (13.5 oz) full-fat coconut milk
- 1/4 cup powdered erythritol (or sweetener of choice)
- 1 teaspoon vanilla extract
- 2 tablespoons coconut flour
- 1 cup shredded coconut (unsweetened), divided

For Topping:

- Additional shredded coconut, toasted (optional)
- Whipped coconut cream (optional)

Instructions:

1. Make the Crust:

- In a food processor, combine shredded coconut, almond flour, powdered erythritol, melted coconut oil, and a pinch of salt.
- Pulse until the mixture resembles coarse crumbs and sticks together when pressed.
- Press the mixture firmly into the bottom and sides of a 9-inch pie dish to form the crust. Place in the refrigerator to chill while you prepare the filling.

2. Prepare the Coconut Cream Filling:

- In a saucepan, combine the full-fat coconut milk, powdered erythritol, and vanilla extract.
- Heat over medium-low heat, stirring constantly, until the mixture is smooth and slightly thickened.
- Whisk in the coconut flour and continue to cook for another 2-3 minutes until the mixture thickens further.
- Remove from heat and stir in 3/4 cup shredded coconut. Let the filling cool slightly.

3. Assemble the Pie:

- Pour the coconut cream filling into the prepared pie crust, spreading it out evenly.
- Sprinkle the remaining 1/4 cup shredded coconut over the top of the filling.
- Chill the pie in the refrigerator for at least 4 hours, or until set.

4. Serve:

- Before serving, you can optionally top the pie with toasted shredded coconut or whipped coconut cream.
- Slice and serve chilled. Enjoy this delicious no-bake coconut cream pie!

Notes:

- Make sure to use full-fat coconut milk for a rich and creamy filling.
- Adjust the sweetness of the filling by adding more or less powdered erythritol according to your taste preference.
- For a decorative touch, toast some shredded coconut in the oven until golden brown and sprinkle over the top of the pie before serving.
- Store any leftover pie in the refrigerator, covered, for up to 3-4 days.

This no-bake coconut cream pie is a delightful dessert that's easy to make and perfect for coconut lovers. It's creamy, coconutty, and wonderfully refreshing. Enjoy making and savoring this delicious pie on any occasion!

Mango Lime Sorbet

Ingredients:

- 3 cups ripe mango chunks (fresh or frozen)
- Zest and juice of 2 limes
- 1/2 cup water
- 1/3 cup granulated erythritol (or sweetener of choice), adjust to taste
- Optional: Fresh mint leaves for garnish

Instructions:

Prepare Mango:
- If using fresh mango, peel and chop the mango into chunks. If using frozen mango, thaw slightly.

Blend Ingredients:
- In a blender or food processor, combine the mango chunks, lime zest, lime juice, water, and granulated erythritol.
- Blend until smooth and creamy, scraping down the sides of the blender as needed. Taste and adjust sweetness if needed by adding more sweetener.

Chill Mixture:
- Pour the mango lime mixture into a shallow dish or container. Cover and place in the refrigerator to chill for about 1-2 hours until very cold.

Churn Sorbet:
- Once the mixture is chilled, transfer it to an ice cream maker and churn according to the manufacturer's instructions until it reaches a sorbet-like consistency. This usually takes about 20-30 minutes.

Serve or Freeze:
- Serve the mango lime sorbet immediately for a soft-serve consistency, or transfer it to a container and freeze for an additional 1-2 hours for a firmer texture.

Garnish and Enjoy:
- Serve the mango lime sorbet in bowls or glasses, garnished with fresh mint leaves if desired.
- Enjoy this refreshing and tangy sorbet as a delightful dessert or palate cleanser!

Notes:

- Adjust the sweetness and tartness of the sorbet by varying the amount of sweetener and lime juice according to your taste preference.
- If you don't have an ice cream maker, you can pour the blended mixture into a shallow dish, cover it with plastic wrap, and freeze it. Every 30 minutes, use a fork to stir and break up the mixture until it reaches the desired sorbet consistency.
- Store any leftover mango lime sorbet in an airtight container in the freezer for up to 1-2 weeks. Allow it to soften at room temperature for a few minutes before scooping and serving.

This mango lime sorbet is a perfect dairy-free and refreshing treat, ideal for hot days or as a light dessert after a meal. It's bursting with tropical flavors and is sure to be a hit with friends and family. Enjoy making and savoring this delightful sorbet!

Sugar-Free Banana Bread

Ingredients:

- 2 cups almond flour
- 1/4 cup coconut flour
- 1 teaspoon baking soda
- 1/2 teaspoon baking powder
- 1/4 teaspoon salt
- 3 ripe bananas, mashed
- 3 large eggs
- 1/4 cup coconut oil, melted
- 1/4 cup unsweetened almond milk (or any milk of choice)
- 1 teaspoon vanilla extract
- 1 teaspoon cinnamon (optional)
- 1/2 cup chopped walnuts or pecans (optional)

Instructions:

Preheat Oven: Preheat your oven to 350°F (175°C). Grease a 9x5-inch loaf pan or line it with parchment paper.
Mix Dry Ingredients: In a large bowl, whisk together almond flour, coconut flour, baking soda, baking powder, salt, and cinnamon (if using). Set aside.
Combine Wet Ingredients: In another bowl, mash the ripe bananas using a fork or potato masher. Add eggs, melted coconut oil, almond milk, and vanilla extract. Mix until well combined.
Combine Wet and Dry Ingredients: Pour the wet ingredients into the bowl with the dry ingredients. Stir until just combined. Fold in chopped nuts if using.
Bake: Pour the batter into the prepared loaf pan, spreading it out evenly.
Bake: Bake in the preheated oven for 45-55 minutes, or until a toothpick inserted into the center comes out clean.
Cool and Serve: Allow the banana bread to cool in the pan for 10-15 minutes, then transfer it to a wire rack to cool completely before slicing.
Slice and Enjoy: Slice the sugar-free banana bread and enjoy it plain or with a spread of nut butter or sugar-free jam.

Notes:

- Make sure to use ripe bananas for natural sweetness. The riper the bananas, the sweeter your bread will be.
- You can customize this banana bread by adding chocolate chips, dried fruits, or seeds to the batter.
- Store any leftover banana bread in an airtight container at room temperature for up to 3 days, or in the refrigerator for longer freshness.

This sugar-free banana bread is moist, flavorful, and perfect for those looking to reduce their sugar intake without sacrificing taste. Enjoy this healthier version of a classic banana bread!

Avocado Key Lime Pie

Ingredients:

For the Crust:

- 1 1/2 cups almond flour
- 1/4 cup melted coconut oil
- 2 tablespoons powdered erythritol (or sweetener of choice)
- Pinch of salt

For the Filling:

- 3 ripe avocados, peeled and pitted
- 1/2 cup fresh key lime juice (regular lime juice can be used if key limes are not available)
- Zest of 1-2 limes
- 1/2 cup powdered erythritol (or sweetener of choice), adjust to taste
- 1/4 cup coconut cream
- 1 teaspoon vanilla extract

Optional Topping:

- Whipped coconut cream
- Lime zest for garnish

Instructions:

Prepare the Crust:
- Preheat your oven to 350°F (175°C). Grease a 9-inch pie dish.
- In a bowl, mix together almond flour, melted coconut oil, powdered erythritol, and a pinch of salt until well combined and crumbly.
- Press the mixture evenly into the bottom and up the sides of the pie dish to form the crust.
- Bake for 10-12 minutes, or until lightly golden. Remove from the oven and let it cool completely.

Make the Filling:

- In a food processor or blender, combine the peeled and pitted avocados, fresh key lime juice, lime zest, powdered erythritol, coconut cream, and vanilla extract.
- Blend until smooth and creamy, scraping down the sides as needed. Taste and adjust sweetness by adding more powdered erythritol if desired.

Assemble the Pie:
- Pour the avocado lime filling into the cooled crust, spreading it out evenly.
- Smooth the top with a spatula.

Chill and Serve:
- Place the pie in the refrigerator to chill for at least 2-3 hours, or until set.

Optional Topping:
- Before serving, top the pie with whipped coconut cream and sprinkle with lime zest for garnish.

Slice and Enjoy:
- Slice the avocado key lime pie and serve chilled. Enjoy this creamy and refreshing dessert!

Notes:

- Ensure the avocados are ripe and creamy for the smoothest filling texture.
- Adjust the sweetness and tartness of the filling according to your taste preference by varying the amount of powdered erythritol and lime juice.
- Store any leftover pie in the refrigerator, covered, for up to 2-3 days. The filling may oxidize slightly over time but will still be delicious.

This avocado key lime pie is a unique and delightful dessert that's dairy-free, sugar-free, and bursting with fresh lime flavor. It's perfect for anyone looking for a healthier dessert option or those following a low-carb or keto lifestyle. Enjoy making and savoring this delicious pie!

Chocolate Almond Flour Waffles

Ingredients:

- 1 1/2 cups almond flour
- 1/4 cup unsweetened cocoa powder
- 2 tablespoons granulated erythritol (or sweetener of choice)
- 1 teaspoon baking powder
- Pinch of salt
- 3 large eggs
- 1/4 cup unsweetened almond milk (or any milk of choice)
- 2 tablespoons coconut oil, melted
- 1 teaspoon vanilla extract
- Sugar-free chocolate chips (optional, for extra chocolatey goodness)

Instructions:

Preheat Waffle Iron: Preheat your waffle iron according to manufacturer's instructions.
Mix Dry Ingredients: In a mixing bowl, whisk together almond flour, unsweetened cocoa powder, granulated erythritol, baking powder, and a pinch of salt.
Combine Wet Ingredients: In another bowl, whisk together eggs, almond milk, melted coconut oil, and vanilla extract until well combined.
Combine Wet and Dry Ingredients: Pour the wet ingredients into the bowl with the dry ingredients. Stir until smooth and well combined. If the batter seems too thick, you can add a bit more almond milk to reach the desired consistency.
Cook Waffles: Lightly grease the waffle iron with coconut oil or cooking spray. Pour the batter onto the preheated waffle iron, spreading it out evenly. Sprinkle some sugar-free chocolate chips on top if desired.
Cook According to Iron Instructions: Close the waffle iron and cook the waffles according to the manufacturer's instructions, typically for about 3-5 minutes or until the waffles are golden brown and cooked through.
Serve and Enjoy: Carefully remove the chocolate almond flour waffles from the waffle iron and serve warm. You can top them with sugar-free syrup, whipped cream, fresh berries, or additional chocolate chips.

Notes:

- Adjust the sweetness of the waffles by adding more or less sweetener according to your taste preference.
- These waffles are best served fresh and warm from the waffle iron but can be stored in an airtight container in the refrigerator for a few days. Reheat in a toaster or oven before serving.
- Customize the waffles by adding chopped nuts, coconut flakes, or your favorite low-carb toppings.

These chocolate almond flour waffles are a delightful treat for breakfast or brunch, especially for those following a gluten-free or low-carb lifestyle. Enjoy making and savoring these delicious and indulgent waffles!

Raspberry Coconut Milk Ice Cream

Ingredients:

- 2 cans (13.5 oz each) full-fat coconut milk, chilled in the refrigerator overnight
- 1/2 cup powdered erythritol (or sweetener of choice), adjust to taste
- 1 teaspoon vanilla extract
- 1 cup fresh or frozen raspberries
- Optional: Chopped dark chocolate or chocolate chips

Instructions:

Chill Coconut Milk: Place the cans of coconut milk in the refrigerator overnight to allow the cream to solidify at the top.
Prepare Raspberries: If using frozen raspberries, thaw them slightly. If using fresh raspberries, rinse and pat them dry.
Make Ice Cream Base:
- Open the chilled coconut milk cans and scoop out the solid coconut cream into a mixing bowl, leaving behind any watery liquid.
- Add powdered erythritol and vanilla extract to the coconut cream. Use a hand mixer or whisk to whip the mixture until smooth and creamy.

Blend Raspberries: In a blender or food processor, blend the raspberries until smooth.
Combine Ingredients:
- Gently fold the raspberry puree into the whipped coconut cream until well combined. If desired, swirl the mixture to create a marbled effect.
- Optionally, fold in chopped dark chocolate or chocolate chips for added texture and flavor.

Churn Ice Cream (if using ice cream maker):
- Transfer the mixture to an ice cream maker and churn according to the manufacturer's instructions until it reaches a soft-serve consistency.

Freeze:
- Transfer the raspberry coconut milk ice cream to a freezer-safe container.
- Cover and freeze for at least 3-4 hours, or until firm.

Serve and Enjoy:
- Remove the ice cream from the freezer a few minutes before serving to soften slightly.

- Scoop into bowls or cones and enjoy this refreshing and dairy-free raspberry coconut milk ice cream!

Notes:

- If you don't have an ice cream maker, you can pour the blended mixture into a freezer-safe container and stir it every 30 minutes until it reaches the desired consistency.
- Adjust the sweetness of the ice cream by adding more or less powdered sweetener according to your taste preference.
- Store any leftover raspberry coconut milk ice cream in the freezer, tightly covered, for up to a few weeks.

This raspberry coconut milk ice cream is creamy, fruity, and perfect for a dairy-free and low-sugar dessert option. It's a delightful treat to enjoy during warm weather or anytime you're craving a refreshing dessert. Enjoy making and savoring this homemade ice cream!

Vanilla Bean Cheesecake Bites

Ingredients:

- 8 oz (225g) cream cheese, softened
- 1/4 cup powdered erythritol (or sweetener of choice), adjust to taste
- 1 teaspoon vanilla extract
- Seeds scraped from 1 vanilla bean pod (or use 1 additional teaspoon of vanilla extract)
- 1/4 cup heavy cream or coconut cream
- Optional toppings: Fresh berries, melted sugar-free chocolate, chopped nuts

Instructions:

Prepare Cheesecake Base:
- In a mixing bowl, beat the softened cream cheese until smooth and creamy.
- Add powdered erythritol, vanilla extract, and the seeds scraped from the vanilla bean pod. Mix until well combined.

Add Cream:
- Gradually add the heavy cream or coconut cream to the cream cheese mixture. Beat until the mixture is smooth and creamy. Adjust sweetness to taste by adding more powdered sweetener if desired.

Chill Mixture:
- Place the cheesecake mixture in the refrigerator for about 30 minutes to firm up slightly.

Form Cheesecake Bites:
- Using a small cookie scoop or spoon, portion out the chilled cheesecake mixture and roll it into small balls using your hands. Place the cheesecake balls on a parchment-lined baking sheet.

Optional Toppings:
- If desired, you can roll the cheesecake bites in chopped nuts, drizzle with melted sugar-free chocolate, or top each bite with a fresh berry.

Chill and Serve:
- Chill the vanilla bean cheesecake bites in the refrigerator for at least 1 hour to firm up further before serving.

Enjoy:

- Serve these delightful vanilla bean cheesecake bites chilled. They make a perfect bite-sized dessert or snack!

Notes:

- For best results, use softened cream cheese at room temperature to ensure a smooth and creamy texture.
- Adjust the sweetness of the cheesecake bites to your liking by adding more or less powdered sweetener.
- Customize these cheesecake bites with your favorite toppings such as shredded coconut, cocoa powder, or a sprinkle of cinnamon.
- Store any leftover cheesecake bites in an airtight container in the refrigerator for up to 4-5 days.

These vanilla bean cheesecake bites are creamy, decadent, and packed with vanilla flavor. They are great for satisfying your sweet cravings in a healthier way, especially for those following a low-carb or keto lifestyle. Enjoy making and savoring these delicious treats!

Lemon Coconut Energy Bites

Ingredients:

- 1 cup almond flour
- 1/2 cup unsweetened shredded coconut, plus extra for rolling
- Zest of 1 lemon
- 2 tablespoons fresh lemon juice
- 1/4 cup coconut oil, melted
- 2 tablespoons honey or maple syrup (adjust amount to taste)
- 1/2 teaspoon vanilla extract
- Pinch of salt

Instructions:

Mix Dry Ingredients:
- In a bowl, combine almond flour, shredded coconut, and lemon zest. Mix well.

Add Wet Ingredients:
- Add lemon juice, melted coconut oil, honey or maple syrup, vanilla extract, and a pinch of salt to the dry ingredients. Stir until a dough forms.

Chill Dough (Optional):
- If the dough is too soft to roll, place it in the refrigerator for 15-20 minutes to firm up.

Form Energy Bites:
- Take small portions of the dough and roll them into balls using your hands. The size can vary based on preference, but aim for bite-sized balls.

Roll in Coconut:
- Roll each energy bite in additional shredded coconut to coat the outside.

Chill and Serve:
- Place the lemon coconut energy bites on a tray or plate and refrigerate for at least 30 minutes to set.

Enjoy:
- Once chilled, these energy bites are ready to enjoy! Store any leftovers in an airtight container in the refrigerator for up to a week.

Notes:

- You can customize these energy bites by adding other ingredients like chopped nuts, seeds (such as chia or hemp seeds), or dried fruit.
- Adjust the sweetness to your liking by adding more or less honey or maple syrup.
- These energy bites are perfect for a quick snack or on-the-go fuel. They are also great for satisfying sweet cravings in a healthier way.

These lemon coconut energy bites are delicious, refreshing, and packed with natural flavors. They make a perfect snack or dessert option, especially for those following a gluten-free or paleo lifestyle. Enjoy making and savoring these delightful energy bites!

www.ingramcontent.com/pod-product-compliance
Lightning Source LLC
LaVergne TN
LVHW081457060526
838201LV00057BA/3061